D0229818

For the
coffee-pourers,
order-takers,
concept-creators
and breakfast-makers.

BREAK FAST

Bianca
Bridges

LON

Where
Real
Londoners
Eat

DON

EBURY
PRESS

Introduction

Key Symbols

I started Breakfast London as an Instagram page to celebrate my love for breakfast, and my love for London.

I'd worked in the food industry and written an award-winning food blog reviewing restaurants, coffee shops and bars, so for me, it was another opportunity to combine my interests of food and social media. Breakfast London's Instagram page quickly attracted other breakfast lovers, building a strong community connected through a mutual adoration of the morning meal. The page was no longer mine, but ours – it became a way for other breakfast- and brunch-goers to share and discover the best spots and dishes in the city.

Unsurprisingly, breakfast has always been my favourite meal of the day. Bacon and egg sandwiches were my kryptonite growing up; stacks of pancakes were (and still are) my go-to hangover cure, and omelettes got me through my university degree. Today, vegan breakfasts are what excites me – experimenting with flavours, textures and combinations using only plant-based ingredients surprisingly presents almost endless culinary possibilities, while being considerate to the world.

I love the way breakfast in London reflects the city itself: the boundless diversity of options and its blend of cultures. Londoners are blessed with the opportunity to experience flavours from all corners of the world in their own city, many of which are manifested in family recipes passed down and perfected for generations. At the same time, British favourites such as fry ups have been part of our breakfast culture for centuries, and can be found at high-end restaurants and greasy spoons alike. We're also seeing a fusion of traditional dishes and global influences, brought to life by utilising quality local and seasonal produce.

This book is a celebration of my personal favourite breakfasts and brunches, influenced by top picks from my friends in the London food scene, as well as eateries selected by Breakfast London's community. It wasn't easy to narrow it down – there are plenty of other spots some would argue also deserve to feature, and of course such is the fast and exciting pace of London that more incredible spots will continue to open long after this book is published.

My mission is always to guide people to have the best possible experiences, while bringing attention to a variety of excellent independent restaurants and cafés that are often overlooked, and to bring together in one place the diverse, innovative and constantly evolving food offerings in my favourite city, my home.

@ @BreakfastLondon
⊕ breakfastlondon.co.uk

Key Symbols

Vegan Friendly

This symbol signifies that the venue is particularly good for vegans, or effort has been made to include a thoughtful plant-based option. However, the majority of eateries will be able to cater for vegans – there might be an option on the menu, or they might be happy to take out and substitute elements to veganise a dish, so be sure to check or ask.

Weekend Only

You won't find any breakfast or brunch dishes here on weekdays. Check the website for current opening hours.

Dog Friendly

This means that all well-behaved dogs are welcome inside the venue. Anywhere with tables outside is usually happy for you to sit outdoors along with your four-legged friend, and some places will allow small dogs inside, so it's worth double-checking with individual spots before you go.

The west central area is known best for its shops and shows – Covent Garden bustles seven days a week with avid shoppers and workers, while the neighbouring district is dubbed 'Theatreland' for its cluster of West End theatres, with buzzing cafés and restaurants woven throughout the streets. Fast-paced and full of energy, King's Cross at the postcode's northern boundary sees Londoners, commuters and tourists, who come and go even before the sun rises, stop for coffee and morning fuel at one of the countless coffee shops nearby. Breakfast is essential before battling through the crowded streets and heaving city hotspots.

Store St Espresso • The Black Penny • The Delaunay • Jacob the Angel • MAMIE'S • Timberyard • 26 Grains • Lundenwic • Half Cup • Abuelo • Patisserie Deux Amis

Store St Espresso

54 Tavistock Place
WC1H 9RG

storestespresso.co.uk

Store St Espresso is a local institution in Bloomsbury. One of the first wave of speciality coffee shops, the team opened up their first site in 2010 with a simple mission: to use the best ingredients possible, for both food and coffee and to prepare everything with care and precision. A laid-back ambience makes this casual yet spacious café an ideal spot for solo coffee missions, meetings and those with laptops.

As one of few coffee operators in central London that remain 100 per cent independent, you can expect a high level of authenticity and personable service. Although the menu is small, they ensure that what they do, they do properly. The team bake everything in house with a focus on flavour and quality, and work with recognised suppliers such as Clarence Court for eggs, MW Capture for smoked salmon and Yeast Bakery for sourdough bread. Must-try dishes include the thick banana pancakes and the garlic roasted mushrooms with avocado.

Store St Espresso's original store is located just a few streets away, but their Tavistock Place site is the only one that offers a breakfast menu.

14

The Black Penny

34 Great Queen St
WC2B 5AA

theblackpenny.com

As soon as The Black Penny unlocks their doors, coffee lovers queue for their morning caffeine hit, and tables fill up with breakfast meetings and tourists alike. Their inviting ethos is partly inspired by the first wave of coffee houses in England in the 1600s, that were nicknamed 'Penny Universities', because whoever you were, all you needed was a penny to allow you to buy a coffee and join in with the intellectual conversations of the day.

The space highlights the building's historic features, such as diamond vault doors and a centuries-old stove-place surrounded by exposed brick and wood panelling. A long centre counter is where the action happens: coffees (by The Roastery Department who roast a bespoke blend) are made here, and an open spread of yoghurt, granola and cake are temptingly on display. Popular menu items include The Hunter (The Black Penny's version of a full English, with eggs however you like), The Gatherer (the veggie counterpart) and the crispy duck hash, as well as the mouth-watering brioche French toast seen widely on social feeds.

➡

The Delaunay

55 Aldwych
WC2B 4BB

thedelaunay.com

Special occasions, meetings to impress and spoiling yourself – it seems like The Delaunay was created for mornings like these. The 'old-world' design and décor at this grand European all-day café–restaurant in Covent Garden pays homage to the cafés of Vienna and Paris, allowing you to feel transported back to some indefinite point in the nineteenth century.

The restaurant prides itself on a quality of service and food that befits the grand setting. The Delaunay truly believes that breakfast is the most important meal of the day, and their breakfast menu is a nod to this. The 'Bakery Breakfast' offers a selection of viennoiserie and sourdough toast with preserves and spreads and a choice of hot drink to accompany it, while the 'Viennese Breakfast' is comprised of smoked ham, salami, artisan Gouda, a boiled egg and rye bread. There are also plenty of British classics, such as two boiled eggs with soldiers, however the showstopper is the oatmeal soufflé with a rhubarb and apple compote, which requires twenty minutes to prepare.

Adjacent to the restaurant, you'll find The Delaunay Counter – a traditional Viennese café serving tempting hot drinks and viennoiserie to either eat in or take away, as well as freshly prepared breakfasts.

Jacob the Angel

16½ Neal's Yard
WC2H 9DP

jacobtheangel.co.uk

There are a few ways to know if a café is probably going to be great. If it's the sister café to The Barbary and The Palomar, it's undoubtedly worth visiting. When you know it's named after the first coffee house in England – opened in 1651 by a man called Jacob – you'll expect big things from the coffee.

And you'd be right to. Square Mile supplies the café's coffee beans, and with a mighty fine coffee machine and trained baristas in the mix, Jacob the Angel know a thing or two about a good cup of morning fuel.

'What we wanted to do is really good coffee, and really good stuff to go with coffee,' explains Daniela Gattegno, who was Head Chef at the café when it first opened.

Inside the cosy space you wouldn't immediately guess that everything, from their cookies to signature tahini madeleines, is baked in house. Jacob the Angel often experiment with new items and recipes, switching up their menu offering depending on what's popular. If you're lucky, you may catch one of their previous standout bakes on sale, a coffee shop staple – muffins. Expect a counter filled with both sweet and savoury muffins, with varying flavours

(I 6 ½)

JACOB

the

ANGEL

* * *

AN ENGLISH

COFFEE

HOUSE

Mon-Fri	Sat-Sun
8 AM - 5 PM	9 AM - 5 PM

and blends of ingredients. The sweet muffins generally come in familiar flavours (blueberry, lemon and ginger), but the savoury ones are more adventurous – expect unusual combinations such as sweetcorn, green chilli and spring onion.

Other breakfast options include lighter granola dishes and a small selection of cooked breakfasts. The customer favourite, however, is their perfected Jerusalem bagels filled with smoked trout and cream cheese.

The coffee shop is ideal for take-aways enroute to work, and those who have time to grab a seat can sip steaming cups of coffee and people watch as they stare out on Neal's Yard.

MAMIE'S

19 Catherine St
WC2B 5JS

mamies.co.uk

Located in Covent Garden, MAMIE'S
is a true Breton crêperie, which strives
to bridge the gap between Breton and
British culture. The team specialise in
both traditional sweet crêpes and galettes,
their savoury cousin made with a crispier
and healthier buckwheat-based batter,
which is also gluten-free. The buckwheat
flour is imported straight from Brittany
from the Moulin de Charbonnière – a
mill that has specialised in buckwheat
flour since 1923.

Brittany is France's north-west
peninsula, where a proper meal is
constituted of traditional galettes for
mains and delicious crêpes for dessert,
served with cider.

This homey and cosy crêperie
feels like a trip to Paris or Brittany.
The restaurant has three different and
unique floors. The secret basement (their
cidrothèque, meaning 'cider cellar') is
decorated with a painted glass ceiling of
a magnificent 1680s map of Brittany. Sip
on French ciders while reclining on the
club-like felted upholstery. The ground
floor showcases an open kitchen for
customers to observe crêpiers at work,
and the first floor is the traditional 'Salon
Breton' with textured, pastel-coloured
walls and stained mirrors.

The menu consists of a range of
different flavours and fillings, with an
option to design your own creation, and
breakfast can be enjoyed as a sit-down
meal or an on-the-go morning treat.
Customer breakfast favourites include
the classic *complète galette* (egg, ham and
emmental cheese) and the banana and
Nutella crêpe. If you're in need of an
additional sugar fix, enjoy with MAMIE'S
popular hot caramel drink, prepared with
milk and homemade salted caramel.

Timberyard

7 Upper Saint Martin's Lane WC2H 9DL

tyuk.com

If you're searching for a café where you can sit with your head buried in a laptop or book, Timberyard is the place. The café was designed to be a hub for freelance workers who can instantly feel at home amongst like-minded creatives. It's a destination for laptops and meetings, and the perfect spot in central London to sit at all day, fuelled by food and cups of coffee (The Roastery Department). It's unsurprising that a large number of Londoners have scanned the buffet of baked goods sprawled out on the counter at least once or twice, and so many can call Timberyard their regular hangout.

Set over two floors, comfortable chairs and sofas for working or relaxing create a little piece of quiet in the bustling city. The café provides plenty of plug sockets for laptops and phone chargers alike, and there are rooms available to hire for meetings or conferences.

Breakfast is served all day on weekdays, and the more extensive weekend brunch menu is served until 3pm. The creamy coconut porridge, granola bowl, and avocado toast with a sprinkle of chilli remain solid customer favourites.

26 Grains

1 Neal's Yard
WC2H 9DP

26grains.com

Initially born as a porridge shop, 26 Grains has grown into a space that embodies everyday casual dining, serving food that isn't dissimilar from what you'd cook at home. Each and every recipe served at the café has come from someone in the 26 Grains team, or the kitchen of Alex Hely-Hutchinson, 26 Grains' founder. That way, they just prepare simple, honest food that they like to eat.

That being said, porridge still plays a central role in 26 Grains' seasonal menu. The team considers a lot when creating each bowl of porridge, from how to layer crunch against the creamy oats, to revolving menu items around the seasonality of fruits. A customer favourite, as well as Alex's top choice, is the hazelnut butter porridge.

'I lived in Copenhagen and suddenly discovered that putting butter on porridge was a bit like putting butter on toast. It is so good and delicious when you've got salty, creamy oats with a little bit of butter,' swoons Alex.

Another of the dishes that reminds Alex of Copenhagen is the Nordic pear porridge, inspired by a time in her life that was filled with glögg, cardamom buns and ginger tea.

Alex started in the food industry working for a granola and cereals company before deciding she wanted to be more involved in the process of making food, rather than the sales and production side. 'If I'm honest, I really didn't know if this was going to fly,' she admits. However, her love of porridge, together with the thought of meeting like-minded people along the way, helped her take the leap to start working for herself.

Tucked away in the oasis of Covent Garden's Neal's Yard, the cosy café is filled with regulars who routinely order their go-to morning dish, small groups catching up over warm bowls and London explorers looking for a quick break from the bustling city surrounding them. 'Breakfast is such a funny service because everyone is kind of sleepy, but it's the time of day that I find you have the most regular habits. So no matter how many times you change the menu … someone will come in, and they will be here every single day eating their hazelnut butter [porridge] because that is their thing, that is their routine,' says Alex, who appreciates how special it is seeing familiar faces during the café's breakfast service.

26 Grains work with many London-based suppliers including Brick House Bakery, HG Walter, Assembly Coffee Roasters, Good & Proper Tea and The Estate Dairy. They also use organic whole oat groats, which they split and soak themselves before cooking – similar to a coffee roastery roasting their own coffee, or a bakery milling their own bread – keeping the kernel intact to achieve 26 Grains' renowned creamy, delicious consistency.

Nordic Pear Porridge

From 26 Grains

SERVES 1

½ cup rolled oats
½ cup nut milk (coconut
    milk or almond milk)
½ cup water
pinch of salt
⅛ tsp cinnamon
⅛ tsp vanilla
⅛ tsp ground
    cardamom
⅛ tsp ground ginger
⅛ tsp turmeric
1 tsp maple syrup
1 pear, cored and chopped
1 tsp raisins
1 tsp mixed seeds
coconut yoghurt, to serve

Best eaten in an oversized jumper on a chilly morning, all it takes is one steamy mouthful to realise why this is one of the most popular bowls in the porridge-focused café. Side effects include internal warmth and convincing yourself that you're actually Danish.

Mix the oats, nut milk, water and salt in a saucepan and start to warm over a medium heat. Then add in all the spices.

Keep stirring the porridge, allowing it to infuse with the spices, for 5–10 minutes. Once you've got it to a porridge-like consistency, take it off the heat and pour into a bowl. Drizzle with the maple syrup and then add chopped pear, raisins and mixed seeds. Serve with coconut yoghurt on top.

Lundenwic

45 Aldwych
WC2B 4DW

lundenwic.com

A minimalist coffee shop set in contrast to the neighbouring chains in the heart of Theatreland, Lundenwic serve freshly baked goods, basic all-day breakfast dishes and speciality coffee roasted by Assembly in Brixton.

The menu is concise but offers something for everyone, from buttery croissants to moreish cheese toasties, with an emphasis on take-aways. Breakfast go-tos include avocado on sourdough with chives, lemon zest and paprika (make it your own by adding halloumi or a fried Clarence Court egg), and for a sweet option, the toasted banana bread with blueberries and pistachio.

Lundenwic's small-yet-sufficient theme is also reflected in the cosy store size – yet it still manages to offer a quick escape from the bustling surroundings of theatres, offices and nearby tourist attractions. Just around the corner you'll find Somerset House, and you can walk over Waterloo Bridge for views of the London Eye and St Paul's Cathedral with a coffee in hand.

Lundenwic also has a location in Spitalfields.

Half Cup

<u>**100–102 Judd St**</u>
<u>**WC1H 9NT**</u>

halfcup.co.uk

Half Cup knows how to do brunch, and they serve it seven days a week, until 3.30pm in the afternoon. With an extensive menu, bold flavours and stunning presentation, the café is a must-visit for those looking for a morning meal packed with sunshine, or to up their Insta-game courtesy of their photo-worthy plates. The charcoal breakfast brioche bun – filled with grilled bacon, smashed avocado, rocket and egg (fried, scrambled or poached) – is a customer favourite. For those visitors craving something sweeter, the Oreo French toast is decadent and delicious, dressed with Nutella mascarpone, crushed Oreos and berries, and is sure to be food-envied by surrounding tables.

Mornings get busy quickly, but cheerful staff and walls with hand-painted murals help to maintain the café's colourful and bubbly vibe. For busy days, pop in for a coffee (Nude Coffee Roasters) and muffin to go, and on sunny ones grab a seat at one of their tables outside.

Abuelo

26 Southampton St
WC2E 7RS

abuelocafe.co.uk

An Antipodean-meets-South American coffee house and kitchen, Abuelo hosts a relaxed space with all-day dining in the heart of Covent Garden. The café was launched by a mother–daughter team with Argentinian and Australian heritage.

The breakfast menu combines family recipes with global ingredients, all beautifully presented and destined to feature on social feeds. The kitchen create innovative and unusual brunch dishes, like the huevos divorciados de turco (poached eggs with salsa roja, salsa verde, avocado and labneh) and honey-whipped mascarpone with fresh figs, crushed salted pistachios and edible flowers on toast.

Coffee is taken just as seriously as the food while also reflecting the heritage of the owners; Abuelo combines South American beans with Australian coffee techniques to provide an impeccable coffee experience.

Although cosy and low-key, the strikingly designed café is photo-worthy, influenced by the similarities between the Australian homestead and the South American haçienda. Check out the walls adorned with landscape paintings, and be sure to say hello to Annie, Abeulo's house dog. ➡

36

Patisserie Deux Amis

63 Judd St
WC1H 9QT

Patisserie Deux Amis feels like a little drop of Paris in London town. A petite French-style patisserie in Bloomsbury, highlights include their flaky, buttery croissants and the drool-worthy apricot Danish pastry – best eaten while sat outside reading a newspaper with a steaming espresso.

On the display counter, visible through the large, picturesque shopfront window, you'll also find tempting fresh baguettes and other baked goods to take away. Inside, you'll find a cosy tea room inviting you to take a break from the city streets.

An ideal pitstop for visitors to London, Patisserie Deux Amis is near to attractions such as The British Museum, The British Library and The Charles Dickens Museum.

Mornings don't get much better than sipping and socialising at a slower pace than usual by Regent's Canal, beside which plenty of cafés and restaurants have set up shop. From Stoke Newington to Barnsbury, popular neighbourhood coffee shops and breakfast spots are filled with local families and residents on weekdays, while weekends invite queues of hungry brunch voyagers. Freshly baked goods also play a strong role in north London's breakfast scene, with hand-rolled bagels, sourdough loaves and specialised pastries catching the eye of Londoners and city visitors alike.

The Barge House • **The Haberdashery** • Banner's • **Brunswick East** • Esters • **The Good Egg** • Franks Canteen • **Fink's Salt & Sweet** • Tina We Salute You • **Café Beam** • 100 Hoxton • **St Paul Islington** • Sunday • **Towpath** • Toconoco • **Friends of Ours** • Black Axe Mangal • **Pophams Bakery**

The Barge House

46A De Beauvoir Crescent
N1 5RY

bargehouse.co.uk

Although The Barge House serves breakfast daily, their weekend-only 'Breakfast in Bread' – a hollowed out sourdough loaf packed with breakfast favourites – has been a sensation on social media. The restaurant now makes over 300 a day with various fillings, from 'The Original', packed full of smoked bacon, a Barge House banger, slow roasted tomato, leeks, oyster mushrooms and spinach, topped with a free-range egg and cheese, to 'Hot Stuff', filled with chorizo and hot beans among other elements. There's also a vegetarian and vegan version.

Everything is cooked fresh, and the loaves are baked by nearby Better Health Bakery, a social enterprise that provides trainee placements to adults recovering from mental ill health.

Although housed in a new building set on the stunning Regent's Canal, the site was originally a print house for porn magazines. Debbie, a funeral director who wrote and conducted bespoke farewells for the Great Train Robber's funerals, runs the bar. Her husband Fred, a recording engineer who has worked with the likes of Bob Dylan, The Prodigy and David Gray, created the menu. He doesn't consider himself a chef, but a great cook.

The Haberdashery

22 Middle Lane
N8 8PL

the-haberdashery.com

When two friends who had tired of the usual high street chains wanted to create somewhere warm, welcoming and community-focused, just like one might find in Sydney, Vancouver or Cape Town, they built The Haberdashery.

Located in Crouch End, the homey café and garden was restored from an old Victorian shop. The furniture and servingware is mismatched and vintage, and the food is freshly made and seasonal. The team bake large amounts in house, including their bread and muffins served in photo-worthy garden pots.

The Haberdashery takes pride in supporting their community by sourcing many ingredients locally, including meat from the butcher on their street and tea from a hundred-year-old family business nearby. Even their halloumi is freshly made on a dairy farm in Barnet.

The breakfast menu is packed with sophisticated comfort foods, highlighting a strong representation of vegetarian and vegan dishes. Be sure to order a hot chocolate, sourced from an old family business in the Dolomite mountains in Italy, served in a bowl.

The Haberdashery has a second location in Stoke Newington.

➡

Banner's

21 Park Rd
N8 8TE

bannersrestaurant.com

Banner's has been a Crouch End institution since 1992. The menus are all about global, hearty home cooking, combining Jamaican flavours, Cajun-style elements and British greasy spoon classics.

The standout breakfast dish is the Jamaican breakfast, with ackee, bacon, boiled eggs, spicy beans, hash browns and warm traditional roti (vegetarian version available). Mexican influences are evident in the spicy bean and manchego cheese quesadilla, as well as Indian in the 'Old Bombay' burrito, which consists of scrambled eggs, coriander, paprika and coconut sambal wrapped in a South Indian paratha. A traditional fry up is also on the menu.

Crayons, books and specialised menus are at the ready in this family-friendly restaurant, and fresh juices, smoothies and milkshakes are also available in children's portions.

The décor is eclectic, with dark wood, brightly coloured furniture and bits and bobs hanging on the walls, including old movie posters and tribal masks. There's also a plaque on the bench where Bob Dylan sat when he visited in 1993.

Brunswick East

Unit 3D Stamford Works
Gillett St
N16 8JH

brunswickeast.london

At Brunswick East mornings last until
the kitchen closes, because they believe
brunch is the best meal of the day. An
Antipodean café in Dalston, it's run by
Natasha Bacon and Shaunae England,
sisters who grew up in a suburb in
Victoria, Australia that the café is fittingly
named after. In true Australian fashion,
Brunswick East specialises in coffee and
brunch. 'We put 100 per cent of our
efforts into coffee, into brunch, and to
make it bloody good. We want people to
sit down and go "yes!",' affirms Natasha.

After a spontaneous decision to open
the café, Natasha and Shaunae sought
to offer brunches like those in Australia.
Their colourful menu is focused on
making dishes a little bit special, a little
bit interesting. 'You'll never find a full
English breakfast on our menu . . . We
like creativity, I think it's really important,'
Natasha explains. Favourites include
the chilli poached eggs with potato
sourdough, wilted spinach, whipped
garlic yoghurt and chilli and dill butter
(which Shaunae claims she could eat
every day) and the 'Vegan Dreaming'
– potato sourdough topped with
homemade beetroot relish, avocado,

46

confit mushrooms, watercress and a mixed seed salad with homemade coriander and cashew cream.

The café has a very strict 'No Shit Egg' rule, and understandably take eggs very seriously, which is reflected in the menu. The detail considered for each and every dish is evident when noting just how much they make in-house: jams, relishes, nut milks and cauliflower toast amongst other items. It can also be seen through their hand-picked suppliers, such as Dusty Knuckle Bakery, Alchemy Coffee and Newington Green for fruit and vegetables.

Located by Gillett Square, Brunswick East's courtyard is frequented by brunch-hungry Londoners, especially on a sun-filled weekend. Inside, the café is spacious and is manned by friendly folk who will happily accommodate as many people as they can squeeze in. For newcomers, the place is on the trickier side to stumble upon. But nonetheless, it wasn't difficult to win hearts. 'I just think it's the most wonderful place. It's a space for everybody, it's inclusive, there are all walks of life that exist on that square. Being here is wonderful,' says Natasha.

Esters

55 Kynaston Rd
N16 0EB

estersn16.com

Esters is a neighbourhood spot nestled on a cosy back street in Stoke Newington, where regulars are on first-name terms with staff and every customer is treated warmly. The café specialises in exciting, seasonal breakfasts and make as much as they can in-house, including jams, yoghurts, pickles and cakes.

Owned and run by Nia and Jack, the couple met working at Fernandez & Wells before starting their own venture. Mornings are their favourite time; starting off slowly with customers seeking coffee and breakfast before work, and picking up later with families, freelancers and four-legged friends. The team change up the breakfast menu regularly, but you'll always find sourdough toast (from Little Bread Pedlar) with homemade preserves and pumpkin seed butter, Bircher muesli with a seasonal compote, a version of French toast, and a fried or poached eggs dish with varying accompaniments.

Esters is light and airy, with bold colours creating a unique space. They also have a courtyard out back for sun-seekers, where herbs and even a fig tree are grown. Payment is card only. No menu alterations, and no laptops allowed on weekends.

The Good Egg

93 Stoke Newington Church St N16 0AS

thegoodegg.co

The Good Egg's menu is influenced by the cuisine cooked by the Jewish diaspora around the world – from the food sold at Tel Aviv street markets to the Jewish deli scenes of Montreal and New York.

Their signature shakshuka with preserved lemon yoghurt, sourdough toast and either crispy halloumi or spicy hogget merguez is a mainstay, and the sabih – an Iraqi aubergine pita with tahini, mango amba, dak dak, pickles and zhoug – is also popular, either to eat in or take away. On weekends, pair with a brunch cocktail like their pastrami-spiced Bloody Mary named 'Red Hot'.

The interior and furnishings are also reflective of their North American and Middle Eastern influences. The restaurant's architectural forms are reminiscent of 1920s Tel Aviv, while their wooden benches take inspiration from those in New York's Utica Avenue Station, and open shelving was designed to provide the feel of a Montreal or NYC Jewish deli, with a bulk of their dry stock on display.

The in-house bakery makes pastries and cakes daily, including the Insta-famous babka, as well as hand-rolled Montreal-style bagels and flatbreads.

The Good Egg has a second location in Soho's Kingly Court. ➡

Franks Canteen

86 Highbury Park
N5 2XE

frankscanteen.com

Franks Canteen just wants to cook great, fresh food using strong suppliers. A bustling neighbourhood café in Highbury, visitors will find a weekly changing menu that's worldwide in style, along with superb coffee from the team at Dark Arts Roastery.

Living in the area and having operated a wedding catering business, the apparent shortage of decent café options in Highbury pushed Paul Warburton to open Franks Canteen, something he knew would appeal to the locals. Midweek carries a relaxed vibe, whereas weekends are busy with customers flocking from all around town, prompted by effusive reviews from London-wide publications.

The menu develops through discussing what's in season, or with an idea, that is then adapted to their own style. Classic dishes presented with a modern angle are bestsellers, however the tarka dal, sweetcorn and coriander fritters and the kedgeree are all in high demand when they're on the menu.

Not one for clutter, the space is clean, bright and airy with outside seating.

Fink's Salt & Sweet

70 Mountgrove Rd
N5 2LT

finks.co.uk

Fink's Salt & Sweet is the neighbourhood go-to spot we all want to live around the corner from. With shelves stocked with unfamiliar artisan products and glazed baked goods piled on counters that'll see off any self-restraint you may think you have, the café feels familiar and homely, even on your first visit. Although they're a casual joint with a laid-back vibe, owners Jess and Mat consider every detail, from designing the breakfast menu to hand-picking suppliers and products they stock. 'We do everything ourselves because we're control freaks,' laughs Jess. '[We evolve] based on what's good around here, what we are making, what we're enjoying.'

They're accustomed to the ritual of weekday mornings, with customers shuffling outside before they've even unlocked the doors. 'There's this lovely little frenzy of people who've just dropped their kids to school or are on their way to work late,' Jess states. 'They come in and it's sort of their pre-day social chill out. I just really like it.' Following this, laptops usually appear during a quieter mid-morning, before being met by the lunch crowd.

By Saturday and Sunday, Fink's Salt & Sweet morphs into brunch central. By ten o'clock, there's a queue out the door, and the café is filled with a buzz you'd find only on weekends. Tables are covered with prosecco, Bloody Marys and brunch boards, surrounded by friends, families and well-behaved dogs and children. Food is simple yet innovative, with Jess and Mat often designing dishes around great produce. 'For me, it's always about finding interesting people and the stuff they make, and making it work in the menu,' says Jess.

Eggs Salt & Sweet

From Fink's Salt & Sweet

SERVES 2

50g salted butter
2 of the tastiest tomatoes you
    can find, thickly sliced
a splash of Balsamic vinegar
a healthy glug of olive oil
6 free-range eggs
2 tbsp mayonnaise
4–6 rashers of unsmoked
    streaky bacon
4 English muffins (or
    2 poppy seed bagels)
salt

This isn't your average egg sandwich. With the delicious addition of snap-crisp bacon and brown butter, it is an ideal way to begin mending a hangover.

First of all, make the brown butter. To brown the butter you're looking to burn it – but only just. Go too far and it'll taste charred, get it right and it'll taste nutty, rich and slightly sweet. Heat it in a heavy based pan over a medium heat. Let it bubble and start to foam up. Hold your nerve!

As the foam dies down, the butter will start to give off a nutty smell. Wait a few seconds, remove from the heat and allow to cool.

To make the balsamic tomatoes, cut them into chunky slices, drizzle in balsamic vinegar, olive oil and add a pinch of salt. Then roast in the oven at 180°C/gas 4 until slightly browned.

Now hard-boil your eggs. Cover the eggs with cold water in a saucepan and bring to the boil. Once boiling, remove from the heat, put a lid on the pan and leave for 8–10 minutes, then remove from the water and run under cold water.

Peel off the shells and mash the eggs up with the mayo and a pinch of salt. Discard some of the white before mashing for a creamier, tastier mix. You can fry your bacon, or do it Fink's style by roasting it on a baking sheet until it's snap-crisp. This will take about 30 minutes at 200°C/gas 6, depending on the thickness of your bacon.

Slice the muffins or bagels in half widthways and toast them. Slather with brown butter before assembling – first, top half the muffin/bagel with a spoonful of egg, a layer of balsamic tomatoes and finally the bacon. Sandwich the other half of the muffin/bagel on top – and you're done.

Tina We Salute You

47 King Henry's Walk
N1 4NH

tinawesaluteyou.com

Tina We Salute You is a sunny, corner café with a strong artistic vibe. With regularly changing installations on both its inside and outside walls, its quiet Dalston location allows people to sit outside and relax in the sunshine on warmer London days.

From the moment they open, the café is bustling. Food is a mix of classic breakfast/brunch options, with everything prepared in-house, and coffee is from Alchemy Coffee Roasters. The team change the menu as and when they like, and include different specials most weekends to keep things interesting.

Dishes such as the homemade granola and the breakfast beigel (with Londoner sausage, a fried egg and homemade spicy tomato sauce) have a permanent place on the morning menu. The scrambled eggs with smoked salmon is also popular, made with the excellent smoked salmon supplied by Secret Smoke House in London Fields.

Tina We Salute You has a second location in East Village, Stratford. ➡

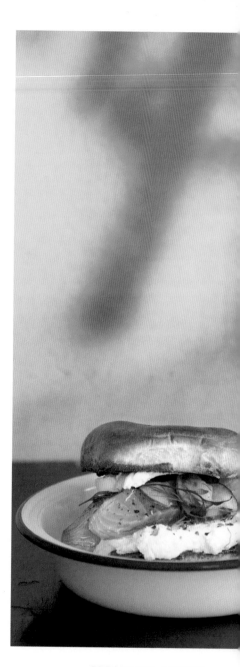

Café Beam

<u>40–41 Topsfield Pond</u>
<u>N8 8PT</u>

cafebeam.co.uk

An independent café run by a local Crouch End family, Café Beam take pride in putting an emphasis on superior ingredients and food. With five chefs housed in a large kitchen, the team is dedicated to producing brunch dishes of the highest standards, in large, wholesome portions that never skimp on quality.

Mornings attract families and laptop-workers alike, in need of breakfast and a cup or two of coffee. The menu weaves classics such as the full English breakfast and French toast (a hot seller at the café) together with globally inspired dishes like their delicious shakshuka (vegan option available). The breakfast burrito and gluten-free buttermilk pancakes are also popular choices amongst hungry brunch-goers.

Café Beam's attention to quality can be seen through their choice of suppliers, including Allpress coffee, meat from Smithfield Market and Galeta pastries.

Café Beam have a second location in Highbury.

100 Hoxton

100–102 Hoxton St
N1 6SG

100hoxton.com

(SAT SUN)

Everything about 100 Hoxton seems on trend. This starts with the warehouse-esque industrial-chic interior, featuring whitewashed walls with wooden panelling, hanging pendant lights, emerald bar stools and a steel bar in the centre of the room. There are also a handful of tables outside the restaurant for al fresco brunching on warmer days.

The restaurant's Asian influences are less evident on the weekend-only brunch menu, but can be seen in options like the koroke Korean croquette with poached eggs, chilli dressing, crispy bacon and cheese sauce, as well as the cured salmon with cornbread, scrambled egg, wasabi yoghurt and herb salad. But generally, Western dishes feature more heavily on Saturday and Sunday, like the 100 Hoxton big breakfast – pork belly, onion hash, fried eggs, tomato and avocado salsa, mushrooms, toast and jalapeño.

Bottomless brunch is a key focus at 100 Hoxton, featuring Aperol spritz, prosecco or boozy slushies to accompany your morning meal.

St Paul Islington

<u>274B St Paul's Rd</u>
<u>N1 2LJ</u>

stpaulislington.com

Located seconds from Highbury and Islington Station, St Paul Islington is a neighbourhood favourite. An all-day destination bistro, they offer up grab-and-go breakfasts for those wanting a quick pit stop, with pastries and a flat white providing a solid kickstart to any day.

For those with a little more time on their hands, the breakfast menu lists familiar yet well-executed options, such as filled croissants with ham and cheese or Nutella and banana, and hot crumpets swimming in butter. Highlights include the smoked salmon with scrambled eggs on sourdough, chorizo baked eggs and the avocado smash with chilli. Team it with a coffee (Caravan) or fresh juices.

A Victorian frontage with wide picture windows allows the spot to be drenched in sun, and offers a stellar view for people watching. The patisserie counter takes centre stage, tempting customers as soon as they walk through the door.

St Paul Islington take reservations during weekdays, however Saturday and Sunday see a walk-in only policy.

←

Sunday

169 Hemingford Rd
N1 1DA

Sunday is a neighbourhood café in Barnsbury, whose food has given them the status of a must-visit brunch destination. On weekdays the café is filled with families and local residents, but the weekends bring a crowd from further afield, keen to travel for the breakfast dish spotted on their social feeds. Even a forty-five-minute queue for a table doesn't deter their determination to try the all-day weekend brunch, and when it comes to their stack of buttermilk pancakes topped with honeycomb butter, berries and maple syrup, you can understand why.

The café is owned and run by Alan and Terry, friends who have been cooking together for years. Not only do they create the breakfast dishes, but they also cook and work at the café full time. They produce original and constantly changing breakfast dishes, inspired by ingredients and cuisines from around the world, which they then make in their own Sunday style.

Aside from the pancakes, fixed menu items include their corn fritters, brioche French toast and Welsh rarebit with smoked haddock, which have become Sunday classics. Other dishes are talked through, created and put on the menu, sometimes all in the space of two hours. 'That's the beauty of having your own kitchen, we're able to do that,' says Alan. 'If we want to put something on, we can do it.'

Sunday endeavours to use as many local suppliers as possible. With vegetables from Newington Green, meat from Godfrey's in Highbury and coffee sourced from Caravan, the café not only maintains great relationships with their suppliers, but makes a point to support other businesses nearby.

Towpath

42 De Beauvoir Crescent
N1 5SB

Towpath is the epitome of simple, memorable food made with quality ingredients. Closed during the winter months, it is a prime spot during the summer with both indoor seating and outdoor space in which to soak up the sunshine along Regent's Canal. The charming setting, along with the friendly and laid-back vibe, has gained the café a cult-like following amongst north and east Londoners and those happy to travel a little further.

Visitors order the daily offerings at the counter from chalkboard menus. Expect unpretentious options like toast with jams, fried eggs on toast, cheese toasties and granola with yoghurts and berries.

You won't find much about them online – their blog has a single post from 2010 (the year they opened) – and pretty much all coverage comes from visitor's blogs and review websites.

Chat amongst friends, people watch or daydream next to the canal, but be wary of pedestrians and cyclists on the towpath.

Toconoco

28 Hertford Rd
N1 5QT

toconoco.com

A family-friendly Japanese café, Toconoco (a made-up Japanese word that means 'kids on the floor') is a calming and minimalist space that overlooks Kingsland Basin on the Regent's Canal.

The café was designed to feel like an extension of your living room, and a homemade ethos is evident throughout. The furniture is bespoke – all hand-built by the owner – and individual cups, mugs and pots have been created by commissioned artists in Japan and the UK. With no signage outside, Toconoco stays simple: the main decoration is the view of the water through the window and the people who join them inside. The staff are kind and the food is well-priced.

Toconoco doesn't consider itself a restaurant, but instead a canteen like those commonly found in Japan. Start your morning with toast topped with the likes of avocado wasabi or egg miso mayo, or even Japanese spreads such as matcha butter, red bean pesto and black sesame butter. Try one of their five Japanese tea lattes, alongside a rice ball (or two).

Friends of Ours

61 Pitfield St
N1 6BU

friendsofourscafe.com

Friends of Ours focuses on three things: great brunch, great coffee and great service. 'We try and offer all three things to anyone who comes in,' explains Anthony, owner of the café. Inspired by his experience of brunch cafés in Melbourne, there's a definite Australian influence embodied in not only the ethos, but also the café's menu. 'We're kind of inspired by the Aussie brunch in how they just pick menu items from all around the world,' he says. With a constantly evolving seasonal menu, they do just that, featuring Asian dishes and Spanish brunches alongside Mexican favourites.

Located not far from Old Street Station and off a cycle superhighway, the considerate bike racks outside and friendly staff indoors exude an inviting level of warmth. Regulars are not only on first-name terms with the staff, but their daily coffee order has been memorised, as well as what they got up to on the weekend. For less frequent visitors, the team are just as welcoming. With the addition of their spectacular coffee (supplied by Dark Arts Coffee) and colourful food, it's easy to see why London sightseers include the café on their itinerary.

Weekday mornings start with a flurry of take-away trade, with customers nipping in for a croissant and coffee, followed by those wanting cooked breakfasts appearing slightly later on. Weekends, on the other hand, are all about brunch. Bloody Marys sit amongst photo-worthy plates, before they're demolished and posted online.

Black Axe Mangal

156 Canonbury Rd
N1 2UP

blackaxemangal.com

On Highbury Corner roundabout,
Turkish food meets heavy metal at this
rebellious restaurant where diners sit in
close proximity as old-school rock blares.
Features of the cosy site include the
large pizza oven decorated with a KISS
tribute and tablecloths that are louder
than the music playing.

   You don't forget a meal at Black
Axe Mangal. Admittedly, the weekend
-only brunch is comprised mostly
of lunch-based dishes, with only a
couple of breakfast-y items making
an appearance on the menu. But,
though few in number, when the
more traditional breakfast ingredients
(think scrambled eggs, hash browns)
do find their way onto the perfectly
orchestrated plates, it's definitely worth
shouting about.

   On the short, explosive menu, you
might find salivate-worthy dishes like
crispy pigs' cheeks, hash browns and
oozy spicy eggs, or Vietnamese scrambled
eggs with bacon and shrimp. The varying
selection of flatbreads are a must-order,
with the squid ink and smoked cod's roe
version sprinkled with glitter being
a customer favourite.

Pophams Bakery

19 Prebend St
N1 8PF

pophamsbakery.com

In a city full of skilled bakers and mouth-watering pastries, Pophams Bakery stands out with their inventive flavour combinations, indulgent options and exceptional quality. Breakfast here is coffee (Ozone) and viennoiseries only, but after the immediate smell of freshly baked pastries hits you as you walk in, you'll be unable to think of anything else.

The menu is ever-changing, and founder Ollie and the team work hard at refining, improving and continuously creating. However, you'll always find options such as the bacon and maple croissant on the menu – a customer favourite where the bacon is baked first to crisp up the fat; baked again inside a laminated spiral pastry, which is then painted with maple syrup to sink inside the layers and coat the salty bacon. Seasonal specials are equally tempting – usually custard-based with added fruits and nuts, like the strawberry and basil custard, and the nectarine and ginger custard.

On weekdays, Londoners inhabiting this work-centric area are constantly moving, with breakfast baps taken away and steaming coffees sipped on the go. Eateries – both situated on the ground and high up in city sky-scrapers – are filled with early breakfasts and morning meetings run by suits and creatives alike. City explorers are also wandering early, visiting iconic London destinations such as St Paul's Cathedral and the Tower of London before the larger crowds pour in.

The Modern Pantry • **Polo Bar** • Ozone Coffee • **Bourne & Hollingsworth Buildings** • Caravan • **Look Mum No Hands!** • Ask for Janice • **Attendant** • Duck & Waffle • **Hawksmoor Guildhall** • Good & Proper Tea

The Modern Pantry

<u>47–48 St John's Square</u>
<u>EC1V 4JJ</u>

themodernpantry.co.uk

'The Modern Pantry is really all
about mixing things up a bit,' says
Anna Hansen, Head Chef. 'It's about
traditional dishes with a twist, which is
applicable throughout the day, especially
at breakfast.' Dishes like the pancakes
topped with smoked ricotta and a berry
liquorice compote, or the sugar-cured
prawn omelette, which are both popular
choices on the morning menus. For
those looking for something a little more
familiar from the extensive options, the
restaurant also serves up classics like
boiled eggs (organic, free-range from
Rookery Farm) with buttered Vegemite
soldiers and lighter dishes such as
porridge and Bircher muesli, alongside
an assortment of pastries.

Keeping things interesting comes
naturally to Anna, a Kiwi from Auckland.
New Zealand's café culture, as well as
Anna's Danish mother and a father
living in Canada, have all influenced her
style of cooking and contributed to her
flawless ability to unite ingredients and
redesign classic breakfast dishes.

Great coffee is also something Anna
describes as essential to her and to The
Modern Pantry. Theirs is supplied by
fellow Kiwis from Caravan, who the

restaurant has been using since Caravan first started their roastery operation.

The attractive Grade II listed brick building stands out on St John's Square in Clerkenwell, with large windows and black and gold signage. While on weekday mornings it's mostly filled with people having meetings, the weekend brunch is a bit more special. The service feels more relaxed, people take their time and – Anna says – are more adventurous with what they order, many of them having travelled some way for the great brunch at The Modern Pantry.

Polo Bar

176 Bishopsgate
EC2M 4NQ

polo24hourbar.co.uk

True to their website URL, Polo Bar really is open twenty-four hours a day, seven days a week. You can get your eggs whether it's as the sun rises, for supper, or at 3am after a night in town. In fact, the only day they actually close is Christmas Day, where they have to board up the entrance because they don't have a door.

Located opposite Liverpool Street Station, Polo Bar was established in 1953 by current owner Philip Inzani's Auntie Bruna. Philip saw potential in the place, which was originally only on the ground floor, so he bought the rest of the building, rebranded it, and still doesn't pretend it is anything other than a great British café. Offering homemade food, the café sees all sorts of characters dining with them throughout the never-ending day.

Breakfast is served all day and is by far the most popular meal. Weekday mornings see take-aways and office deliveries of bacon baps, bacon and egg baps, bacon and avocado baps, and so on. Of course, they do plenty of other breakfast sandwiches and melts without bacon, but it seems to be the bacon that everyone wants. In fact, the restaurant gets through 250kg of bacon a week, which means they are able to have it specially dry cured to order.

Although their traditional full English is the most popular dish, Polo Bar also has a dedicated vegan menu. With an aim to make sure every customer is happy, they'll also create bespoke requests if you don't find what you want – although this feels quite unlikely considering the amount of menu options. From healthy plates to award-winning pancakes, calendar specials and even the occasional food challenge, you'll never leave hungry.

Ozone Coffee

11 Leonard St
EC2A 4AQ

ozonecoffee.co.uk

The team behind Ozone are coffee specialists, who have put roasting and serving coffee at the heart of what they do.

The Old Street space houses a wholesale roasting operation, a retail coffee offering and a full-scale restaurant. The highly functional space uses hard-wearing materials like steel, concrete and zinc, contrasted with soft industrial lighting. Lush greenery also appears alongside constantly changing artwork.

Doors open at 7am and it doesn't take long for the morning masses to start filling the space, including four-legged early risers (check out their hashtag #dogsofozone).

The menu is a nod to their Kiwi roots, focusing on sustainable and whole-cycle cooking. A signature brunch dish is the Kumara fry-bread with herbed avocado, smacked cucumber, sumac yoghurt and a poached egg. Elements of the dish change with seasons, however the fry-bread, based on the traditional Maori fried bread, remains the same. Another classic Ozone breakfast is eggs benedict served on bubble and squeak cakes with hollandaise.

Coffee lovers can experience a variety of flavours and choice of brewing methods. Espressos are prepared with Ozone's flagship espresso blend, Empire, and they showcase single-origin coffees on their full soft brew bar. If you're looking for something with a bit of a kick, the Ozone Bloody Mary with kimchi salsa is a weekend winner.

Bourne & Hollingsworth Buildings

42 Northampton Rd
EC1R 0HU

bandhbuildings.com

Bourne & Hollingsworth Buildings is strikingly good-looking.

There are various areas that make up B&H, including the café and private dining room, both bright and easy on the eye. However, the most picture-perfect of them all is the Greenhouse, adorned with an abundance of lush greenery, whitewashed brick walls and natural light. Marble tables are surrounded by colourful floral seats, mismatched yet fitting together. This leads into the Garden Room, the largest restaurant space, with similar décor.

Weekend brunch sees pancake variations, poached eggs (most popularly the lobster royale and huevos benedictos – with chorizo, avocado, béarnaise sauce and pico de gallo), as well as other breakfast classics. Brunch cocktails are a must, especially with a bottomless option, otherwise sip on cold-press juices or kombucha.

Dogs are welcome in the bar area only.

Caravan

11–13 Exmouth Market EC1R 4QD

caravanrestaurants.co.uk

Caravan's restaurants are all about the way people like to eat and enjoy food. The diverse menus weave their way around the world, showcasing various flavours and influences from the founders' home country, New Zealand, and their global travels.

Founded by Laura Harper-Hinton, Miles Kirby and Chris Ammermann, the trio met while working at a restaurant in Wellington and became quick friends as they drank tequila at the bar after shifts. They embarked on a BOE (Big Overseas Experience) together and all ended up in London where they discovered a gap in the market for a relaxed restaurant with 'well-travelled' food and good coffee.

Their first site in Exmouth Market opened in 2010. Coffee drinkers, laptop workers and brunch-goers alike enjoy the energy and buzz of the space. As soon as Caravan opens, queues for morning coffees form beside the bar, while tables start filling up inside and out.

Breakfast and brunch play a key role at Caravan, with classics such as cornbread served with chipotle butter, lime and fresh coriander, a dish that has featured on the menu since day one. It's been said that their chefs have prepared so much of the cornbread that they can make it with their eyes closed. The kimchi pancake with slow-cooked pork belly and fried duck eggs also never fails to impress.

Although well known for their innovative menus, Caravan is really famous for its coffee. The team roast their own beans at their Roastery HQ in King's Cross, and serve it using specialised brewing techniques, creating spot-on flat whites and breakfast martinis. Caravan also supplies coffee to countless restaurants and cafés throughout the UK and beyond.

Caravan has locations in King's Cross, Bankside, the City and Fitzrovia.

Look Mum No Hands!

49 Old St
EC1V 9HX

lookmumnohands.com

Look Mum No Hands! is the ultimate combination of food and cycling. '[It's a place] where you can come get your bike fixed and have a bit of breakfast while you do it,' says Tom Jones, Head Chef at the café. It's also somewhere you can buy cycling gear, clothing and even cycling-related celebration cards. Since it opened in 2010 as one of the first cycle cafés in the city, Look Mum No Hands! has built a strong reputation amongst London's cycling community for great coffee, beer, food and knowledgeable bike mechanics.

Breakfast-lovers will feel just as comfortable amongst the bikes suspended from the ceiling and cycling artwork – if you're not a cyclist before you go in then you'd definitely be considering it by the time you've left.

LMNH does a great job of the breakfast classics. You can expect variants of a full English breakfast (classic, vegetarian, vegan), eggs benedict and even peanut butter toast topped with banana and berries.

On weekends, breakfast runs until half past two in the afternoon. It gets busy, with inside the café and the large outdoor courtyard by the café entrance filling up with early risers, as well as those who stumble in later carrying hangovers. However, it's never as busy as when there's a cycling event on TV such as Tour de France. Tom admits, 'usually if there's a bike race going on, or even a bike ride starting from here, you'll arrive and there'll be about a hundred cyclists outside and you can't even get in.'

Look Mum No Hands! has a second location in Whitechapel and runs pop-ups around London.

Ask for Janice

50–52 Long Lane
EC1A 9EJ

askforjanice.co.uk

The name Ask for Janice comes from a track in the Beastie Boys' second studio album, *Paul's Boutique*, released in 1989. Ask for Janice is in fact not a boutique, but a laid-back all-day hangout, starting with early breakfast and coffee and closing as a late-night bar where local gin is their thing. On weekends, they're all about bottomless brunch, and brunch-goers can choose three small plates and fill up on Bloody Mary, Buck's Fizz and Salty Dogs.

The breakfast menu is designed to suit both early meetings and lazy weekday brunching. Inspired by seasonal British ingredients and all things eggy, customer favourites include the baked eggs, merguez sausage, roasted peppers and yoghurt, as well as Ask for Janice's legendary homemade crumpets served with seasonal homemade jams.

The space captures the informal, grungy, creative and experimental vibe of New York in the late eighties and early nineties. The interior is filled with works by seminal artists from the early 1990s, such as Damien Hirst and *Kids* director Larry Clark, as well as by contemporary street and graffiti artists including Kid Acne and Pure Evil.

Attendant

<u>74 Great Eastern St</u>
<u>EC2A 3JL</u>

the-attendant.com

Attendant was born with a simple vision: to be a quality brunch café that uses local produce-driven food and serves the highest quality coffee, all sourced both sustainably and ethically. Since the first café opened in Fitzrovia in 2013, two more have followed (Shoreditch and Clerkenwell) and the concept has developed to include a coffee roastery and kitchen.

Attendant's coffee is focused on taste and sustainability when sourced and roasted, ensuring the flavour honours the hard work and efforts put in by farmers and growers. The seasonal breakfast menu gets just as much attention, featuring dishes like the sweet potato smash, house waffles and Maldon smoked salmon (on seeded multigrain toast with porcini and truffle cream cheese) on the menu's 'Hall Of Fame' section.

The Shoreditch site's 'Victorian with a modern twist' interior is photo-worthy. Walls are whitewashed, with eye-catching green bar tiles, hanging plant pots and copper pendant lamps. However, the spot is best known for the living plant wall, which runs the length of the café.

Duck & Waffle

duckandwaffle.com

Duck & Waffle is truly unlike any other restaurant. The setting, on the fortieth floor of Heron Tower, means it has breathtaking views across the city. The lift ride is in itself an unforgettable experience – gaining speed as you watch the ground below you get further away through the glass. This, along with the fact that you can experience this any hour of the day, because Duck & Waffle is a twenty-four-hour restaurant, makes it likely different from anywhere you've been.

Visitors and Londoners alike book in advance to dine in the sky and watch the morning light come over the city, through the floor-to-ceiling windows that surround the restaurant, or to even feel the odd comfort of being surrounded by a cloud of fog. Alternatively, well dressed night owls can visit in the early hours for some drinks and a mix of breakfast and late-night dishes, depending on what you're craving at three in the morning.

Prepared in an open kitchen, the popular breakfast menu is well known amongst London residents, especially the signature Duck & Waffle served with mustard maple syrup. Many of their other dishes have also made a name for themselves, including their sweet waffles

(originally created to share, although many wisely choose not to) and Colombian eggs – a simple yet incredibly satisfying dish of scrambled eggs folded with tomatoes, spring onions and a side of avocado.

Eggs are, of course, a central part of the menu, and are sourced from Cackleberry Farm in the Cotswolds, who are responsible for those orange yolks. With a lot of care for their produce, Duck & Waffle ensure everything is traceable and list details of where ingredients are sourced from on the back of their menus.

Full Elvis Waffles

From Duck & Waffle

A tribute to Elvis Presley's favourite
sandwich – fried peanut butter and banana
– the Full Elvis Waffles is a decadent way
to start any morning. For this recipe, you'll
need a waffle iron and a big appetite.

SERVES 4

1 tin condensed milk

Peanut brittle
100g sugar
50g salted peanuts

Buttermilk waffles
180g flour
10g sugar
1 tsp baking powder
½ tsp baking soda
pinch of salt
180ml buttermilk
35g butter, melted
1 small egg

Chantilly cream
200ml double cream
20g icing sugar
1 vanilla pod

To serve (per waffle)
1 banana
1 tsp caster sugar
1 tbsp strawberry jam
2 tbsp peanut butter
handful of strawberries, halved
handful of raspberries
handful of blueberries
1 tsp cocoa nibbs

Place the tin of condensed milk in a pan of water and boil for 4 hours. Take care to keep topping the pan up as the water evaporates. Then remove from the pan and allow to cool to room temperature. When it's cool, open and transfer the contents to a container ready to use later on. Store in the fridge.

To make the peanut brittle, add the sugar to a small saucepan and add a little water. Place over a low-medium heat until the sugar caramelises to a golden brown colour, then turn off the heat. Now add the nuts and stir in until they are all coated in the caramel. Spread the mixture out on a lined baking sheet and allow to cool. Once it's set hard, smash up with a rolling pin and store in an airtight container.

Now make the waffle batter. Whisk together the flour, sugar, baking powder and soda, and salt in a bowl, then whisk together the buttermilk, melted butter and egg in another bowl. Whisk the liquid bowl into the flour mixture until just combined. The mix will be quite thick, which is perfectly normal. Store in the fridge.

Now whisk the ingredients for the Chantilly cream together until the cream forms stiff peaks.

Heat your waffle iron and cook the first waffle until golden brown, which will take around 4 minutes. In the meantime, peel the banana and split in half lengthways. If you have a cook's blowtorch, sprinkle the sugar over the flat side of the banana and caramelise with the flame. If you don't have one you can skip this step.

When the waffle is ready, take out and onto a plate, smothering it with jam and peanut butter. Next add the banana halves and all the berries followed by a good spoon of the chantilly cream. Drizzle the caramelised evaporated milk sauce all over, then finish with a good pinch of cocoa nibs sprinkled over and some of the peanut brittle. Eat straight away.

Hawksmoor Guildhall

<u>10 Basinghall St</u>
<u>EC2V 5BQ</u>

thehawksmoor.com

Hawksmoor is most famous for its dictionary-thick steaks, however those who are familiar with the Guildhall location will know it's the only one of the restaurants to offer a meat-centric breakfast menu.

The menus revolve around quality ingredients, and the restaurant supports traditional British farming methods, working with small farms around the country who raise cattle to their specific set of guidelines around the quality of the animal's life.

The interior features reclaimed materials throughout that you could easily spend hours discussing. Most spectacularly, walls are lined with solid mahogany panelling made from specimen cabinets from the Natural History Museum; the teak flooring is from the 1920s University of the Arts building (now UAL), and the heavily embossed wallpaper was made traditionally from linseed oil and pulp by a company that made the wallpaper for the first-class cabins on the *Titanic*.

Located beside an iconic building in the City, the 800-year-old Guildhall, home to the Corporation of London, Hawskmoor at breakfast time sees both early meetings and longer indulgent mornings. The decadent breakfast menu features the sausage and egg 'HkMuffin' inspired by McDonald's, as well as the luxurious lobster benedict, comprised of half a lobster and a poached egg sat atop an English muffin and drowned in hollandaise sauce.

However, the menu's focal point is the Hawksmoor breakfast for two, with smoked bacon chop, sausages, black pudding, short-rib, bubble and squeak, grilled bone marrow, trotter baked beans, fried eggs, grilled mushrooms, roast tomatoes, HP gravy, and topped off with unlimited toast.

Hawksmoor Guildhall is closed at weekends but available to hire for events.

Good & Proper Tea

96 Leather Lane
EC1N 7TX

goodandpropertea.com

As tea specialists, Good & Proper Tea are on a mission to show everyone how great tea can be. The knowledgeable team source a variety of whole leaf teas from around the world, which customers can take home as loose leaves or tea bags, in gift sets, or have brewed in store.

Located on the Clerkenwell Road end of Leather Lane, Good & Proper Tea moved into their flagship 'Tea Bar' in 2016 after two years of serving up cups of tea and crumpets out of a converted Citroën-H van around the UK (which they still do).

The core of the breakfast menu is built around Good & Proper's sourdough crumpets with alternating crumpet toppings, based upon what is in season, as well as all of the classics: jam, butter and salt, cheese and marmite, and avocado.

Filled with foliage and tea leaves, painted white walls and English oak structures, Good & Proper Tea is a haven of calm – ideal for weekday breakfasts, early meetings, take-away treats and of course, that perfect cup of tea.

East London is a diverse and eclectic hub of creators, makers and doers. While a surge of fresh and dynamic energy is evident in the area, the old-school East End is kept alive through pubs and greasy spoons, as well as by the strong market culture – mornings at Broadway Market, Netil Market and Old Spitalfields Market are a rush of traders offering a mix of specialised food, produce and goods, with breakfast eaten amongst those browsing and buying. Brunch-goers flock to enjoy contemporary cooking and experimental breakfast combinations seen on many morning menus in the area.

Cereal Killer Café • Pavilion Café • Berber & Q • St. John Bread and Wine • I Will Kill Again • E. Pellicci • White Mulberries • Dishoom • Pacific Social Club • Smoking Goat • MOTHER • Morty & Bob's • Mae + Harvey • The Dusty Knuckle • Treves & Hyde • Lanark • TRADE • Morito • Delamina East • Wood Street Coffee

Cereal Killer Café

139 Brick Lane
E1 6SB

cerealkillercafe.co.uk

Cereal Killer Café is a sugar-rushed (big) kids dream. Forget debating over which box of cereal to choose – you can mix, match, construct your own masterpiece and let your imagination run wild. Not for the indecisive, the café offers over a hundred different types of cereals from around the world, with around thirty toppings to choose from, in addition to a spectacular range of milks. To save time, a tried-and-tested route is available in the form of 'cereal cocktails' – combinations they've created themselves – alongside flamboyant milkshakes and hot chocolates that have likely popped up on your social feeds.

Co-owners (and identical twins) Alan and Gary Keery have cereal for breakfast every day. As youngsters, their mother would take them to the supermarket, allowing them to choose one box of cereal each. 'All the colours and everything, all the different toys you get, and having to choose, that is a very hard decision for a six-year-old,' says Gary.

Transporting nineties kids back to their childhoods, cereal boxes cover the café's walls, while downstairs beds

provide seating ('breakfast in bed') and small televisions blare old cartoons.

'I think the nineties was the best decade for cereal, I think that's when it really peaked,' says Gary. 'That's when you were getting all the exciting flavours and the exciting characters, but I think we've sort of lost it now and there's a lot of people wanting to get back to that, and that's what we can do here.'

Cereal Killer Café has a second location in Camden.

Pavilion Café

Victoria Park
Old Ford Rd
E9 7DE

pavilionbakery.com

On a sunny day, Pavilion Café offers the dreamiest of all settings. The lakeside pavilion is located in Victoria Park, and visitors can eat their morning meal on the jetty as they watch swans cruise past, or sit on one of their communal tables.

Fresh bread, flaky croissants and banana bread loaves are baked by the in-house bakery, and pantry items like their homemade peanut butter are on sale, ensuring you never leave empty-handed.

The meat-free menu features globally inspired dishes, including the Sri Lankan breakfast (with roti, dal, sambal and turmeric egg curry), as well as hearty classics like the veggie breakfast (fried egg, mushrooms, halloumi, avocado, beans and toast). The kitchen also whips up thick, decadent pancakes (with varying toppings) drowning in syrup, which are somewhat Insta-famous.

Weekends are bustling on warmer days, so expect a queue to order inside. Dogs are welcome, but not allowed inside the pavilion.

Berber & Q

Arch 338 Acton Mews
E8 4EA

berberandq.com

Located under a brick railway arch in Haggerston, Berber & Q is a Middle Eastern and North African grill house influenced by the mangal restaurants in Turkey, grill and kebab houses of Istanbul, the food stalls of the huge Jemaa el-Fna market in Marrakesh and shipudiya (grilled meat restaurants) in Tel Aviv.

The brunch offering is a collection of some of co-founder Josh Katz's favourite dishes, discovered whilst travelling abroad and reimagined slightly using his Western viewpoint and influences.

The Full Israeli (for two) is the mouth-watering customer favourite. A tray is filled with a changing collection of the restaurant's favourite mezze along with staples such as soft-boiled eggs, avocado and honey feta cheese, as well as yoghurt topped with hazelnuts, tahini and date syrup. The shakshuka, which can be made for one or two persons, is also a must-order.

St. John Bread and Wine

94–96 Commercial St
E1 6LZ

stjohnrestaurant.com

There's no such thing as a typical morning at St. John Bread and Wine. 'Each morning brings its own adventures,' says Fergus Henderson, co-founder of St. John. Trevor Gulliver, the restaurant's other co-founder, agrees. 'All restaurants are like that. They have their own rhythm and flow, which kind of reflects what's happening outside, whether it's the weather or it's a Saturday.'

With Fergus training to be an architect and Trevor creating merchandise in the rock 'n' roll business, it was a possibility that St. John would not have been born. Their first restaurant, St. John, opened in 1994 and remains in Smithfield, asserting itself to a legendary status in gastronomic circles through 'nose-to-tail' eating. The more casual Bread and Wine bakery and restaurant in Spitalfields opened in 2003, and is famous in its own right.

The site was originally set to be a bakery, but plans had to be changed as it quickly grew into something bigger: 'After four days, Ferg and I looked at each other and said, "Oh dear, we better tell the baker we have a restaurant," because people came in and started sitting down,' Trevor admits.

A few years ago, you would have only found bacon sarnies for breakfast here – though arguably the city's favourite bacon sandwich. 'You can't knock the bacon sarnie,' Farokh Talati affirms, Head Chef at Bread and Wine. 'Bread baked by St. John bakers. Rare breed bacon grilled on our grill, loads of butter, homemade ketchup – it's awesome.'

The team had missed doing breakfast at St. John's hotel in Chinatown, which shut its doors a while back. 'We've always loved breakfast,' states Trevor. 'Fergus gives good breakfast.' Those dishes are now making their way into Bread and Wine. Dishes that are a harmony of quality ingredients, all of which have been detailed to perfection, yet somehow made to seem effortless – like their smoked bacon, haricot beans, tomato and trotter gear (a term coined and made popular by Fergus himself, which is stock made from trotters simmered in water). 'Nice hearty dish to start you off with the day,' says Farokh proudly. They're quite happy to serve a Black Velvet (stout beer and champagne) with your breakfast, and be sure to leave with their famous freshly baked doughnuts in hand.

I Will Kill Again

Arch 216
27A Ponsford St
E9 6JU

darkartscoffee.co.uk

Down a service lane in a railway arch, you'll feel like you're in the wrong place. Only when you've spotted the tables outside and a motorbike or two will you know you've arrived at I Will Kill Again.

The café opened in the Dark Arts Coffee Roastery after the team noticed an increasing number of people turning up to the roastery, wanting to meet the people behind the brand and try the coffee on site. The décor and furniture already existed as it was a hangout for Brad and Colin – the owners of Dark Arts – as well as their friends. A kitchen was built, and I Will Kill Again was born – a Breakfast London favourite.

Each and every cup of Dark Arts Coffee is exceptionally good, and the breakfast dishes match this. I Will Kill Again doesn't follow café trends, and the refined menu focuses on food that you can't simply whip up yourself at home. Although not exclusively a vegan café, there are always a great number of drool-worthy vegan options on offer, including the popular homemade muffin (with za'tar, cream 'cheese', rosti, avocado, smoked tempeh, oven blushed tomatoes and kasundi), as well as a bounty of

vegan pastries including croissants and 'sausage' rolls.

Order at the counter inside, where sofas, chairs, benches and couches invite you to hang out. The interior reflects 1970s motorbike culture, and framed, original *Time* magazine covers picturing serial killers hang on the wall.

Weekends are crazy busy, so come early or expect a wait.

E. Pellicci

332 Bethnal Green Rd
E2 0AG

epellicci.com

E. Pellicci is an iconic East End greasy spoon. Trading since 1900, it's a slice of London's history – so much so that the café was awarded Grade II listing by English Heritage. The custard Vitrolite panelled storefront, combined with the art deco interior that sees marquetry panelled walls hung with family portraits, epitomises caffs from the interwar period.

The menu blends classic British and Italian dishes, and breakfast is comprised of traditional fry ups. Pellicci's full English and its vegetarian counterpart are listed beside a catalogue of other components that you can add, swap in, or create your own masterpiece with. The few other morning options include muesli and yoghurt, and liver, bacon and chips.

Although hearty, comforting and of fantastic value, it's not the food that makes the café special. E. Pellicci is family-run by the friendliest of faces, with Mama Maria in the kitchen while her kids, Nevio Jnr and Anna, and cousin Tony run front of house (read more about their story on their website). The warm hospitality, where guests are treated as members of the loud and laid-back family, plays a prominent role in every experience there.

White Mulberries

D3 Ivory House
E1W 1AT

whitemulberries.com

Mornings around the Tower of London
are a bustle of rush hour commuters and
early-rising tourists. But just a stone's
throw away you'll find St. Katharine
Docks, a calm escape by the water and
the only marina in central London.

Rana runs White Mulberries
alongside her husband Peyman – friends
that fell in love over their mutual dream
of starting a coffee shop. The cosy café
is located in Ivory House, which, built
in 1858, is the oldest of the original
warehouses in St. Katharine Docks, and
comes complete with a view of the docks
that you'd never get tired of.

The seasonal menu, displayed on
a letter board behind the counter, has a
healthy focus. It includes crowd-pleasers,
from avocado on sourdough toast to
scrambled eggs with smoked salmon,
as well as their drool-worthy supply of
freshly baked goods.

Allpress has long been the house
coffee, with their guest coffees constantly
rotating. 'We love working with boutique
roasteries and supporting smaller,
independent roasteries. The baristas
love to try the different coffees, as do
the customers,' says Rana.

←

Dishoom

7 Boundary St
E2 7JE

dishoom.com

Dishoom is a tribute to Irani cafés that were once a large part of everyday living for residents of Bombay – now Mumbai.

Breakfast time at the Shoreditch site can be deliciously lazy, especially if you get a spot on the dog-friendly veranda. Dishoom's menus bring together the very best of Bombay comfort food, while putting their own spin on the breakfast dishes in particular. The famous and highly recommended bacon and egg naan roll is not a traditional Bombay dish, but Dishoom's take on the British bacon butty – Ramsay of Carluke's smoked streaky bacon and Blackdown Hills West Country eggs served in a freshly baked naan with chilli tomato jam and coriander. The 'Big Bombay' breakfast (vegan version available), the Kejriwal (fried eggs on chilli cheese toast) and the keema per eedu (minced chicken topped with fried eggs, sali-crisp chips and served with homemade buns) are also highly recommended.

Aside from the Shoreditch site, there are Dishoom restaurants in Covent Garden, King's Cross, Soho, Kensington and Edinburgh.

Pacific Social Club

8 Clarence Rd
E5 8HB

pacificsocial.club

Pacific Social Club was opened in 2011 by Liam and Nick, as a reaction to Liam being shushed for speaking in a café where everyone was on a laptop. The duo wanted to create a space that was chatty, inclusive and jumbled up to reflect Hackney.

The café is described by the pair as a 'vaguely Pacific-rim oriented, Japanese/Irish café/izakaya/record label/mobile disco/museum hidden away on a Jamaican/Kurdish street.' The décor is an explosion of tropical prints, retro Japanese matchboxes, shop signs and fertility statues, topped off with gramophone record wallpaper and disco light projectors. Yet the vibe is as casual and easy-going as it gets. Laptops and tablets are permitted in the back room, keeping the main café space social.

Breakfast is all about toasties. Highlights include the homemade kimchi, mature cheddar and scallion toastie, and – if you're starving – the Venezuelan sandwich with morcilla, chorizo, chipotle, black beans, avocado and cheese. For a lighter option, the aged gouda with yucatan honey and paprika on toast is a customer favourite. Pair with a horchata ice coffee or a watermelon, sour apple and mint juice.

Smoking Goat

64 Shoreditch High St
E1 6JJ

smokinggoatbar.com

Smoking Goat is a Thai barbecue bar serving Bangkok-inspired breakfast. The restaurant is well known for their interpretations of northern and eastern Thai barbecue dishes, showcasing rare breed meats and day boat fish from small production farmers and fishermen, which guide the menus.

The breakfast menu is focused around freshly made roti – a popular Asian street food flatbread with flaky layers of oiled dough. Smoking Goat use Sous Chef Meedu's childhood recipe, and you can watch the team cook them from scratch on a charcoal skillet in the open kitchen. The roti are served in dishes such as the smoked aubergine, egg and chilli roti, as well as the traditional roti with curry sauce.

Other morning dishes include the brisket burnt ends khao soi northern Thai gravy noodles, transporting you to a part of the world where noodles are eaten for breakfast daily. Order with a sweet Vietnamese-style coffee with condensed milk, a fresh juice or a Thai-style Bloody Mary.

Brunch at the Smoking Goat runs all weekend.

MOTHER

Unit 1 Canalside
Here East Estate
E20 3BS

mother.works

A sanctuary in a big city, MOTHER welcomes all to nourish the mind and body at their loving space in Hackney Wick. The site embodies warmth and nature, with plants filling the room and a vegan menu on offer.

The team behind MOTHER believes that food can and should be both nourishing and healing, which is why the menu is mainly organic and avoids all additives, preservatives and hidden nasties. The smoked 'salmon' and cream cheese bagel made with carrot is as convincing as the real deal and demonstrates just how versatile plants can be. The frozen acai bowl, with the option of creating your own version with a variety of delicious toppings, is another a customer favourite. Breakfast at MOTHER is served all day, every day, so customers can get their avocado on toast fix whether it's early morning or dinner time.

MOTHER is focused on its commitment to the planet, and as part of reducing their impact on the environment, they are aiming to become zero waste.

Morty & Bob's

Second Floor
Netil House
1 Westgate St
E8 3RL

mortyandbobs.com

Morty & Bob's is quite literally hidden, and very much a gem. Customers buzz in to gain entry, and – having climbed two flights of stairs at the back of a creative studio building – you wouldn't necessarily expect what you find: a buzzing café by day (transforming into NT's bar in the evenings) with reaching views across London, serving wholesome comfort food. Full of foliage and celebrating building material (concrete, brick, repurposed wood, neon signs), the café also boasts a terrace overlooking east London's train tracks, adding an extra forty covers on a sunny day.

It all began with Morty & Bob's selling grilled cheese sandwiches out of a street food shack at UK music festivals and at Netil Market, next to their current location. The grilled cheese remains a menu staple, as well as the avocado toast with chilli, feta and pumpkin seeds. Other must-orders are the maple and mustard eggy bread with bacon and fried eggs, if you're lucky enough to catch it on the menu, and the wild mushroom on toast with homemade pesto.

Breakfasts are what Morty & Bob's is all about, with the morning light drenching the café every sunny day. Allpress coffee and free Wi-Fi attracts a working crowd, although weekends are strictly no laptops during brunch.

➡

Mae + Harvey

414 Roman Rd
E3 5LU

maeandharvey.com

People don't tend to visit Mae + Harvey when they're in a rush. They take their time to enjoy the cosy space, where you can relax and experience fresh food made with quality ingredients.

Mae + Harvey started with a focus on juicing, serving fresh carrot, orange and ginger juice early mornings at markets – which are still a favourite at the café. They also make a mean flat white with Allpress coffee.

As soon as the doors open, regulars stop by for their morning coffee and poppy seed roll en route to work. The café is bustling shortly after, with dishes such as the smoked salmon waffles (served with avocado and cream cheese) and the avocado and pickled radish toast being devoured. Be sure to order anything with their homemade bacon jam, which takes the kitchen all day to make.

The café is small, with an even smaller kitchen, and customers often make friends while sharing one of the larger tables. Clean white walls, ash wood and statement tiles contribute to the bright and open space, and the team decorate with fresh flowers weekly.

Mushrooms on Toast with Rocket & Hazelnut Pesto

From Morty & Bob's

SERVES 1

1 knob of butter
60g chestnut mushrooms,
    thinly sliced
60g oyster mushrooms,
    thinly sliced
½ garlic clove, finely chopped
chopped parsley
1 slice of toast
1 egg
salt and pepper

*Rocket and
hazelnut pesto
(makes at least
8 portions)*
40g roasted hazelnuts
100g rocket
50g grated parmesan
    (omit if vegetarian)
150ml extra virign olive oil
juice of 1 lemon
1 garlic clove, grated
pinch of Maldon salt

Mushrooms are often the unsung hero of breakfast dishes, but in this recipe they're the star of the show. The pesto can be subbed with store-bought for those in a rush, but is definitely worth the additional effort – leftovers can also be used for an abundance of savoury dishes.

To make the pesto, place all of the ingredients in a blender or a food processor and blend until the desired coarseness. Each batch varies and sometimes the nuts are extra absorbent – be sure to have more extra virgin olive oil on hand and gently pour in a little at a time if you notice the pesto drying up and sticking to the walls of the mixer. For the leftover pesto, place it in a tightly-sealed jar (like a Kilner jar) with more olive oil and store in the fridge for up to two weeks.

Melt the butter in a small frying pan. When sizzling, add the mushrooms and stir. Add the garlic and season with salt and pepper. Cook until the mushrooms are soft and have taken some colour. Now throw in a good pinch of parsley, stir, take off the heat and spoon on to the toast. Replacing the pan on the heat, add some oil and crack the egg in to fry. When this is done to your satisfaction, remove and lay on top of the mushroom toast. To finish, drizzle over the rocket pesto – some on the mushrooms, some on the egg, some on the plate. Give it all a couple of turns of the pepper grinder and serve.

The Dusty Knuckle

Abbot St
E8 3DP

thedustyknuckle.com

The freshly baked bread at The Dusty Knuckle is exceptionally good. An award-winning social enterprise that trains and employs young people facing financial difficulties, the bakery and cosy café houses open shelves filled with loaves of all sizes (that is, if you arrive before they're all gone), ready to be taken home and thickly sliced in your kitchen.

Breakfast during the week is a small but sweet offering, consisting of perfected pastries and breakfast sandwiches on fresh bread, including the classic bacon/sausage on potato bread, as well as egg with Lincolnshire poacher cheese and pickled chilli on focaccia.

Weekend menus are slightly more extensive, where dishes can be inspired by a single ingredient and evolve into a fully developed recipe through discussions amongst the team. The same can be said for their drinks, and The Dusty Knuckle always feature a cordial on the menu using seasonal fruit.

The team create everything in house, aside from some speciality foods sourced from the highest quality suppliers including cheese from Neal's Yard Dairy and coffee from Ozone Coffee Roasters.

➡

Treves & Hyde

<u>15–17 Leman St</u>
<u>E1 8EN</u>

trevesandhyde.com

It's possible that Treves & Hyde may be one of the most photogenic breakfast spots in London. A restaurant, café and bar under Leman Locke, Treves & Hyde's design has a Scandi feel courtesy of the minimalist layout, light woods and a marble countertop. Pastel pink and yellow colours, as well as lush greenery, provide a clean contrast to the grey materials, and floor-to-ceiling windows allow natural light to stream in.

The colourful breakfast dishes are a treat for the eyes as well as the tummy, and include the chia seeds and passionfruit bowl and thick buttermilk pancakes with berries and a pot of maple syrup. The star of the brunch menu is the baked eggs shakshuka served with charcoal toast. Order with a coffee (Assembly) and pastry.

Treves & Hyde are dog-friendly in the café area only.

Lanark

262 Hackney Rd
E2 7SJ

lanarkcoffee.co.uk

Lanark doesn't mess about. There are no frills here, from the straight-to-the-point website (featuring just the name, and buttons linking to their Instagram, Twitter feed and email), to their narrow interior with worn turquoise floors, which can only squeeze in a handful of people at any one time.

There's no need for trimmings and embellishments, because Greg Boyce and Dom Sherington's energy is focused on what they do best: food and coffee. And the coffee is truly excellent, sourced from a rotation of various roasters, including Alchemy, Square Mile and Dark Arts.

Breakfast dishes consist of electrifying and rebellious combinations, ready to both satisfy you and blow your mind. With quality ingredients at the forefront, menu items change regularly, but expect options like the 'Breakadilla' (corn taco quesadillas with homemade kimchi, Clarence Court eggs and herb lime sauce) and the 'Barn' (haggis, bacon, tomato, peppers and poached egg on sourdough).

The team behind Lanark have also opened Visions Canteen on New Inn Yard, off Shoreditch High Street.

TRADE

47 Commercial St
E1 6BD

trade-made.co.uk

The philosophy at TRADE is to make as much as possible from scratch. From the extensive range of cakes and baked treats, to their signature homemade pastrami and smoked turkey featured in many of the sandwiches, they aim to use ingredients of the highest quality to provide customers with simple yet flavour-packed dishes. What they can't produce themselves, they source from artisanal producers when possible.

TRADE's space is adaptable and works all year round. There's a cosy interior for the winter, while the small terrace and large folding doors invite sunshine in for the warmer months. The service style is informal and laid back both on weekdays and weekends, however Saturday and Sunday sees table service, allowing customers to relax and enjoy the bustling café.

This is an ideal spot for breakfast for anyone heading to Brick Lane Market (on Sundays) and Old Spitalfields Market (every day); try a cortado (from Origin Coffee) alongside scrambled egg on toast with grilled chorizo, or smashed avocado seasoned with lime, feta, mint and chilli.

TRADE has a second location on Essex Road, Canonbury.

Morito

195 Hackney Rd
E2 8JL

moritohackneyroad.co.uk

(SAT SUN)

The only downside of brunch at Morito is that it's weekend only. The restaurant is the second site to the original in Exmouth Market, which was in fact the sister restaurant to Moro (opened in 1997 and famous for embracing tapas without the constraints of cooking Spanish-only dishes).

Morito's influences are drawn from southern Spain, North Africa and the eastern Mediterranean. Menus are constructed daily, and are even (impressively) updated punctually on their website. The traditional Turkish menemen eggs with optional sujuk sausage is tantalising; it's served with toasted bread and the choice of adding an extra kick with the spice plate on each table. Even the homemade granola is decadent, with cardamom, pomegranate, pistachios and a choice between yoghurt, milk and almond milk.

The space blends industrial influences with Mediterranean aspects, with polished concrete floors meeting licks of ocean blue on the walls and contrasting with the marble-topped bar. Light streams in through the large windows, and customers can gaze at chefs at work in the open kitchen.

Delamina East

151–153 Commercial St
E1 6BJ

delaminaeast.co.uk

Following a Thanksgiving pop-up
at Shoreditch House that showcased
owner-chef Limor's turkey and
vegetarian dishes with an Eastern-
Mediterranean twist, Delamina East
(previously Strut & Cluck) was born.

Limor draws on her eclectic
heritage for the menu – she was born
in Tel Aviv to a family with both eastern
European and Middle Eastern origins.
Brunch dishes are wholesome, with
a focus on herbs and spices sourced
from Lebanon, Turkey and Israel.
Eggs are generally the stars of the show,
accompanied by various dishes and
dips and an abundance of pita bread.
Must-orders include their take on the
classic shakshuka, turkey shawarma,
and their Jaffa-Tel Aviv-style brunch,
which combines your choice of eggs
with a selection of seven mazetim (side
dishes and dips) and mixed bread.

With a bright, homely setting and
relaxed vibe, background music plays
a mix of tracks from classic French
chansons to Italian ballads, Israeli
hip hop and French–Arab rap.

*Delamina East has a second location
in Marylebone.*

➡

Wood Street Coffee

Blackhorse Workshop
1–2 Sutherland Rd Path
E17 6BX

woodstcoffee.co.uk

Set inside Blackhorse Workshop, Wood Street Coffee is an independent café and speciality coffee roasters.

Couple Gareth and Clare Reid originally ran a market stall at Wood Street Indoor Market (hence the name Wood Street Coffee), moving on to this permanent site also in Walthamstow. The café space was designed by Turner Prize-winning architects Assemble, who have created an airy and semi-industrial vibe with white peg board walls and coloured accents throughout.

Although breakfast is daily, their weekend Antipodean-inspired brunch menu is slightly more extensive and indulgent. Hit up their bacon and egg sandwich slathered with rosemary butter, or, when it's on the menu, the pork belly benedict with miso hollandaise, which takes three days to prepare.

The team roast their own coffee and always have an espresso, filter and decaf on the go, as well as retail bags of their coffee beans (or ground) to take home.

Sit inside and listen to Bonobo on the stereo, pick a table outside in the yard, or grab a coffee and an almond pain au chocolat to take away.

Beyond the abundance of museums and attractions in the area, there's a strong sense of community within the neighbourhoods of south-east London. Eateries are filled with nearby residents who consider the spots to be their local go-to, while Brockley Market, an award-winning weekly market supporting local producers and traders, has Londoners travelling across the city – a must-visit for breakfast. Peckham is a popular area for contemporary bars, food and nightlife, whilst charming and wholesome Greenwich is the place to grab a coffee and pastry at the food and goods market before strolling around Greenwich Park.

The Full Nelson • Where
The Pancakes Are •
The Watch House •
Aqua Shard • Norbert •
Anderson & Co • Vanilla
Black Coffee & Books •
St David Coffee House •
Heap's Sausages • Mother
Flipper • Coal Rooms •
Brick House • Maggie's

The Full Nelson

47 Deptford Broadway
SE8 4PH

thefullnelsondeptford.co.uk

'It's more fun to eat at a bar than it is to drink in a restaurant,' is the foundation on which The Full Nelson was built. A veggie/vegan dive bar and kitchen in Deptford, the team initially thought the comforting Americana-style food would play a secondary role, however they quickly saw that people visited solely for a meal.

The Sunday-only brunch menu epitomises how a vegetarian/vegan diet doesn't miss out on anything. All dishes have a vegan option and hangover cures come in the form of a Big Poppa brunch roll (beer battered 'sausage' patty, garlic mushrooms, cheese, hash brown and caramelised onions on a brioche bun) and the 'chicken' waffles – Southern-coated seitan on a soft waffle with maple syrup and maple butter. Wash down with a strong filter coffee (Dark Arts) or a killer Bloody Mary.

Low-key and relaxed, the intimate rough-and-ready space is backed with a stellar rock soundtrack from eighties metal to doom and power pop. Sit at one of the few tables or grab a stool at the bar.

The Full Nelson's sister spot is The Waiting Room, also in Deptford.

Where The Pancakes Are

85A Southwark Bridge Rd
SE1 0NQ

wherethepancakesare.com

Where The Pancakes Are is, unsurprisingly, a pancake lover's dream. With some of the best pancakes in the city, the menu is full of sweet and savoury pancakes, Dutch babies (a mouth-watering Yorkshire pudding lookalike served in a pan) and monthly specials. The top secret buttermilk batter recipe took years to develop and perfect, and the restaurant also offers a second batter that's both vegan and gluten free.

The pancake variations are a tribute to global influences: '1000 Greens' was inspired by Ottolenghi recipes, the Welsh rarebit pancakes are a tribute to the classic rarebit on toast, and the American – three pancakes with blueberries, streaky bacon and maple syrup – is plucked straight from a US diner.

Quality ingredients take centre stage, with maple syrup imported from Quebec, and bacon and sausages from Swaledale butchers in North Yorkshire. For those who just can't get enough of their batter, Where The Pancakes Are sell their flour mix in store, so you can cook up fluffy stacks in your own kitchen.

The Watch House

31 Shad Thames
SE1 2YR

thewatchhouse.com

The Watch House got its name from its first site – a nineteenth-century watch house on Bermondsey Street, where guards would keep watch for grave robbers and body snatchers. After opening in 2014, The Watch House grew to have two more sites in Bermondsey Street and Fetter Lane. While all of the sites offer daily speciality coffee (Ozone), pastries (The Snapery) and simple breakfasts, the Tower Bridge site is the only one to offer a full breakfast menu.

Just a two-minute walk from the south side of Tower Bridge, The Watch House is a hotspot for nearby residents and workers as well as exploring tourists, with high volumes of take-away trade. Coffee is served on a wooden board alongside cards with printed details of the specific blend. Weekdays invite a flurry of meetings and laptops, while weekends see brunch-lovers taking it easy.

Breakfast is hearty and accessible, embracing British seasonal brunch ingredients. Menu highlights include the colourful eggs royale with beetroot hollandaise, and pancakes with varying toppings – S'more pancakes with Nutella, oat crumb and marshmallow have previously graced the brunch menu.

Aqua Shard

Level 31 The Shard
31 St Thomas St
SE1 9RY

aquashard.co.uk

Mornings on the thirty-first floor of The Shard are spectacular. With the bustle of London's rush hour below, the glass walls show a different side of the city, where things and thoughts move at a gentler pace. At Aqua Shard, breakfast is undoubtedly the most laid-back service. 'The music is a little more mellow, you've got London just waking up and you can kind of see as all the light comes up. It's quite nice and relaxed,' says Dale Osborne, the restaurant's Executive Chef, referencing the sun rising over the city.

Aqua Shard serves contemporary and seasonal British food, focusing on locally sourced produce, as well as products from around the British Isles. With Borough Market on their doorstep and Bermondsey Market nearby, the kitchen works with small businesses that truly know their trade. Breakfast dishes are a celebration of these British suppliers, with bread from the renowned Bread Ahead Bakery, black pudding sourced from the charcuterie specialists Cannon & Cannon, smoked salmon by luxury producers Lambton & Jackson and fresh fruits and vegetables from Turnips, residents at the Borough Market for nearly thirty years.

Dale's understanding of British cooking makes for a perfect fit with Aqua Shard. They serve classics such as an English breakfast with treacle cured streaky bacon and homemade baked beans, as well as a popular vegetarian version. 'One of my favourites is probably the crab scrambled eggs,' Dale confesses. 'We use lovely Cornish crab and we fold it through some soft scrambled eggs with herbs, and then we do little soldiers with brown crab butter.' Despite not being fond of bananas, he also enjoys the brioche French toast topped with caramelised banana, yoghurt and puffed rice. Then again, it's hard to resist.

Brioche French Toast with Caramelised Banana

From Aqua Shard

SERVES 4

4 eggs
250ml milk
½ pod of vanilla seeds
4 thick slices of brioche
4 tbsp butter
4 bananas
100g icing sugar
200g thick organic yoghurt
100g puffed rice

When you can't make it to The Shard, whip up this decadent brioche French toast at home instead. Topped with caramelised banana, thick yoghurt and puffed rice, it's the perfect breakfast for a special occasion or a lazy Sunday.

Whisk the eggs, milk and vanilla together and pour into a shallow dish. Soak the slices of brioche in the mixture for 1 minute. Now melt the butter in a large frying pan and fry the slices of brioche until golden on each side.

Peel the bananas, cut in half lengthways and sprinkle generously with icing sugar. Using a blowtorch (or place under a grill if you don't have one), burn the sugar on the bananas until it caramelises.

To serve, lay the warm, fried brioche on a plate, top with the banana and a good spoonful of yoghurt. Dust icing sugar over the top and sprinkle with puffed rice.

Norbert

209-211 Mantle Rd
SE4 2EW

norbertrestaurant.com

Situated by Brockley Station, Norbert is a British meets modern European restaurant, where fresh seasonal ingredients are used to create dishes throughout the day.

Previously Noak Restaurant, the new team breathed life into the space with a fresh menu and attentive staff. The restaurant is furnished with simple wooden tables and chairs, and the décor generally doesn't try too hard. The curved brick bar is positioned between the diners and kitchen, surrounded by hanging pendant lights.

Breakfast at Norbert covers the customer favourites such as the full English, which features the traditional elements as well as additions like bone marrow. The veggie counterpart, full Veggie, replaces the meat components with avocado, halloumi and seasonal greens. The menu also includes other classics like buttermilk pancakes, house granola and smashed avocado on sourdough (served with poached eggs and dukkah).

Anderson & Co

139 Bellenden Rd
SE15 4DH

andersonandcompany.co.uk

Anderson & Co's morning menu appeals to adults and children alike, with fresh and seasonal dishes, gluten-free and vegan options, as well as the café classics that you might be expecting to see. The quality ingredients are what brings the breakfast dishes to life, including eggs that are laid in Kent on a Monday and arrive at the restaurant on Thursday, and their butcher Flock & Herd delivers three or four times every week. Standout breakfasts include the çilbir (poached eggs, labneh, chimichurri, chilli butter, sourdough) and sweet potato hash, as well as poached eggs with black rice and avocado.

The café sees many regulars who grab a coffee (Square Mile) and a pain au chocolat or almond croissant to go. For those looking for a table, customers can take their pick on their morning setting, either overlooking the street at the front of the café where they can chat to the staff, or tucked away in a quiet corner of the conservatory.

←

Vanilla Black
Coffee & Books

308 Kennington Rd
SE11 4LD

Bright and light-filled thanks to their large shopfront windows, the stylish yellow and white interior at Vanilla Black is Scandi-influenced. The family-friendly café contains a hidden courtyard with olive trees and lavender and an inviting sofa and fireplace downstairs for the colder months, along with a kids' corner complete with books and toys.

The former bookshop retains its original shelving, and offers an impressive selection of on-trend recipe books and children's literature, as well as gifts for sale. The food is healthy and fresh, and the coffee (Allpress) is arguably the best in the area. Not only is Vanilla Black the coffee shop's name, but it's also their signature drink – a long black with a touch of bourbon vanilla extract.

The morning menu is short and simple, brought to life with beautifully cooked high-quality ingredients. The dishes change reflecting the seasons; and suppliers include the New Covent Garden Market (fruits and vegetables), Lambton & Jackson (smoked salmon), and Clarence Court (eggs).

➡

St David Coffee House

5 David's Rd
SE23 3EP

St David Coffee House is much more than the name suggests (i.e., simply a coffee house). It's a local hangout in Forest Hill, where residents come to meet, socialise or just have some time to themselves over a steaming cup of coffee (Square Mile).

What also sets St David apart from the average coffee house is the delectable and creative brunch dishes. The constantly evolving menu is written on the blackboard over the counter, on which are listed bestsellers like the poached egg, bacon and avocado on sourdough toast with rocket and the classic bacon sourdough bap.

Spread over two floors, customers order upstairs and can take a seat at one of the few tables by the counter, or head down to the more spacious basement. The mismatched mirrors and rocking horse hanging on the wall, as well as the friendly staff, make St David Coffee House all the more lovely.

Heap's Sausages

8 Nevada St
SE10 9JL

heapssausages.com

Heap's Sausages is owned and run by Martin Heap, the creator of the Simply Sausages range. The café creates gourmet sausages, handmade on the premises to eat in or to take home to cook.

Off a Greenwich side street, the adorable café exterior is picture-perfect, painted green with panelled windows and outdoor seating. Inside is just as charming, housing display fridges stacked with a large variety of their gourmet sausages.

Breakfast is an all-day affair, and includes British classics like Mr Heap's Great British breakfast (two sausages, dry cured bacon, baked beans, creamed mushrooms, fried egg and toasted bread), and various breakfast baps with sausages and bacon. Customers can choose from over ten different types of sausages, including a vegetarian sausage that's also vegan, and ideal amongst their several hearty vegetarian options.

Heap's Sausages has a second location in Deptford.

➡

Mother Flipper

Brockley Market
Lewisham Way
SE4 1UT

Mother Flipper ensure 'no patty [is] left unturned to create that mother flippin' goodness'. It's an accurate statement, as Mother Flipper's burgers are undeniably succulent and delicious, and are credited to be some of London's best burgers by countless lists.

The popular street food truck didn't leave mornings untouched, and created the 'Breakfast Muffin': it's a sausage patty from The Butchery (who also trade at Brockley Market), a free-range egg and melted cheese between a toasted, buttered muffin, with the highly-recommended option to add a potato rosti and/or candy bacon. Images of the triumphant stack regularly circulates around social media feeds.

You can find the masterpiece at the outdoor Brockley Market, where Mother Flipper trade on Saturdays only – and expect to wait in a queue. Be sure to keep up to date with their location via their Twitter feed (@MotherFlipperUK) to see where else they're trading.

Coal Rooms

11A Station Way
SE15 4RX

coalroomspeckham.com

The food at Coal Rooms revolves around its large smoker and robata grill, which are key to producing hearty dishes with big flavours and different cuts of meat at the forefront.

Operating within a Grade II listed old train station ticket office, the various areas within the site located beside Peckham Rye Station offer slightly different aesthetic influences – the main dining room has a bright Scandinavian feel, whereas the kitchen and counter dining is a darker and more intimate affair.

Midweek mornings are bustling, serving coffee and pastries to the commuter crowd, while the Saturday-only brunch sees classic dishes with a twist, avoiding the standard avocado on toast. The English breakfast for two is the ultimate hangover cure, which includes smoked jerk goat sausages, smoked pigs head blood pudding and smalec (a traditional Polish preparation for pork lard). Order a bacon sandwich and you'll be asked to choose between cuts of the coffee-cured bacon (streaky, back or both) and offered homemade brown sauce or ketchup in a custard bun.

The team also owns the coffee roastery Old Spike.

Brick House

1 Zenoria St
SE22 8HP

brickhousebread.com

Fergus and Sharmin Jackson love good
bread. This is evident at Brick House,
their award-winning sourdough bakery
and café. Initially born as a wholesale
bakery, supplying the likes of Neal's Yard
Dairy and Duck Soup, Brick House
now opens their doors daily to hungry
customers. The café serves seasonal
menus, utilising their sourdoughs and
other house-made products including
charcuterie, jams, pickles, chutneys and
pastries. Brick House offers weekday
breakfast with a special brunch menu
on weekends, where you can find dishes
like migas – their version of a Spanish
dish that uses stale bread soaked in milk
then fried, served with peppers, onions,
chorizo and a fried egg.

Based in an old electrical warehouse
just off Lordship Lane, the light, airy
space houses the working bakery,
shop and café under one roof. With
whitewashed brick walls, high ceilings
and a utilitarian style interior, the café
has fifty covers seated around long
communal tables and at the bar.

Brick House has a second location on
Blenheim Grove, Peckham Rye.

154

Maggie's

322 Lewisham Rd
SE13 7PA

maggiesrestaurant.co.uk

Maggie's Café and Restaurant is a Lewisham greasy spoon just a short stroll from Lewisham Station. The space gets full quickly with their loyal following of local residents and workers, as well as those who have decided to pay Maggie a visit because they've 'heard good things'. It's a family-run business; Maggie and her husband opened the place in 1983.

Unlike the classic caff, Maggie's has table service. Customers are seated upon arrival (provided that there's no queue!) and friendly staff, or Maggie herself, take your order.

Food is very well priced and traditionally British. Customers can create their own breakfast from over twenty classic fry up components, including liver, tinned tomatoes and bubble and squeak. Breakfast is served all day, enjoyed best with bottomless cups of tea or coffee.

Visitors can eat at tables outside, or in one of the two dining rooms. Exposed brick walls surround yellow and green booth seating, with framed black and white pictures adding to the charm of the space.

The south west contains many of London's most significant historical buildings turned popular attractions, including Westminster Abbey, Buckingham Palace and Big Ben. King's Road and Fulham Road are both popular hubs for old-school and stylish shops, bars and eateries, while the rise of Australian café culture is considered to have started across the river in Clapham, with a flurry of corn fritters and flat whites spreading to the neighbouring areas. The eclectic Brixton Market and Market Row are unlike any other; their arcades bring together communities and cultures while offering a delectable mix of cuisines and goods.

Brickwood Coffee & Bread • Milk • Bean & Hop • Brother Marcus • Flour to the People! • Local Hero • Brooks & Gao • Cut the Mustard • Salon • Flotsam & Jetsam • Regency Café • Senzala Creperie • Tried & True • Café Fleur • Ground Coffee Society • Farm Girl • Chairs & Coffee • Burnt Toast Café

Brickwood Coffee & Bread

16 Clapham Common South Side
SW4 7AB

brickwoodlondon.com

Brickwood Coffee & Bread is one of the original Aussie and Kiwi influenced full table service cafés in London, and one of the best. They represent café culture in its truest form by being a local, approachable and friendly spot for breakfast-lovers. Focusing on coffee (Caravan create a bespoke Brickwood blend), fresh brunches, toasties and pastries made in-house, they bring it all together with a comfortable aesthetic and great soundtrack.

Whitewashed brick walls house their cosy interior, and the small courtyard allows brunch-goers to spend warm mornings in the sunshine.

On the menu, you'll find dishes such as 'The Butcher' (Brickwood's version of a full English), made up with 48-hour fermented organic sourdough, St Ewes eggs, and bacon and sausages from Wicks Manor Farms. Brickwood was smashing avocados long before it became a menu staple; their smashed avo on sourdough

topped with poached eggs and chilli is a customer favourite, especially with added feta, chorizo or both.

Brickwood Coffee & Bread also has locations in Balham, Tooting Market and Streatham.

Milk

18–20 Bedford Hill
SW12 9RG

milk.london

Milk is one of those places that, if you somehow don't already know about, you should. A bustling neighbourhood café south of the river in Balham, Milk serve speciality coffee and produce-led brunches 363 days a year. Weekdays are lively, with good music, food and people. Weekends see a queue, but the 1970s Goodman speaker sets the pace as pancakes and coffees fly out of the kitchen.

Sat on the corner of a mews street, the building is mostly glass and invites natural light inside all day. The space is simple and clean, and comes to life on warm days when the bi-fold doors are open and tables spill out onto the pedestrian street. The Victorian brick walls are whitewashed, and the interior is filled with wooden furniture and items the team have collected.

The brunch menu is eclectic but focused, recreating nostalgic classics in Milk's own style. More unusual is the Kurdish baked eggs with roast butternut squash, feta and crispy sage, served in a pan which remains on the menu to avoid a customer uprising. All dishes are winners, especially the 'Sweet Maria' (sweetcorn fritters, grilled halloumi, kasundi, avocado and lime)

and the hangover cure in the form of 'The Convict' – a proper English muffin stuffed with drycure bacon, sausage, Burford brown egg, poacher hash (American diner-style hash browns covered in cave-aged Lincolnshire Poacher cheese) and hangover sauce, which is a house-made smoked chipotle ketchup. For something lighter, try Milk's homemade granola served with yoghurt parfait, seasonal bramble fruits, jasmine syrup and basil.

Milk has a sister café called Milk Teeth in Tooting Broadway.

Bean & Hop

424–426 Garratt Lane
SW18 4HN

beanandhop.co.uk

Of all the things that Bean & Hop, a neighbourhood café in Earlsfield, do well, three things in particular come to mind: colourful modern brunches, spectacular coffee and a solid selection of craft beer that even non-beer drinkers can't help browsing.

Using local ingredients where they can, the café does their best to source responsibly whilst offering great value. Bean & Hop partners only with suppliers they trust and enjoy working with, including Graham, their 'egg guy'.

The daily breakfast menu blends classic British breakfast items, Mediterranean ideas and Australian style. These influences can be seen in dishes like the 'Sun-dried Brunch', made up of avocado on sourdough toast with a poached egg, sun-dried tomatoes and feta (with an option to add some spicy chorizo). The café also offers daily specials that are often gluten free, veggie or vegan.

Weekdays see 'laptoppers' and local parents, while bustling weekends sees swift-moving queues, with customers seldom waiting more than a few minutes, despite the café's popularity.

Bean & Hop's sister location is Café Tamra on Northcote Road.

Brother Marcus

9 Chestnut Grove
SW12 8JA

brothermarcus.co.uk

Alex Large, Arthur Campbell and Tasos Gaitanos had named their restaurant before they knew they wanted to open one. 'Alex would always tell a story and be like "Oh, my brother Marcus",' chuckled Tasos. 'So we had a name for the business before we had any idea about what we were going to do.'

Metres from Balham Station, mornings at Brother Marcus are a flurry of take-away coffees, open laptops and early morning meetings run by businessmen and local mothers alike. Weekends see a slightly different scene, with hungover twenty-somethings flooding in for brunch and a hangover fix in the form of another cocktail. You're quick to get that homely feel, both inside the café and outside in the spacious courtyard, especially since they've made the majority of furniture with their own hands.

The three guys have been friends since sixth form, and all found themselves unhappy working for other people, so they decided to create something for themselves. With an ethos of 'great food, great coffee and great service', they recognise the importance of having all three under one roof, working closely with suppliers to get the best of produce

and altering the menu seasonally.
'Our food is different to anyone else's
food entirely,' says Tasos proudly.
'With ours, you've got flavours, the
colours, playfulness.'

This playfulness is evident on the
menu, from the flavour combinations to
the irresistible dish names. One of their
top sellers is the 'Sister Special', which
features the holy trinity of breakfast foods:
eggs, bacon and avocado. Alongside
this is the cinnamon French toast called
the Sugar Daddy, and their unanimous
favourite, Bob's Your Uncle, a dish with
pork belly, fried egg and pita bread.

*Brother Marcus has a second location
in Angel.*

Flour to the People!

573 Battersea Park Rd
SW11 3BJ

flour2people.com

The concept of Flour to the People! revolves around sourdough and making as much as possible from scratch. Breakfast and brunch at the restaurant includes fresh baked sourdough, ready for toasting by customers using toasters on their table, before slathering with homemade jam, marmalade or chocolate and hazelnut spread.

The eggs benedict are also special, with the chefs creating their own sourdough crumpets instead of the traditional English muffins, as well as making their own hollandaise. The café even churns their own butter three times a week, using the buttermilk for their drool-inducing pancakes.

Although the café is small, it packs a punch. The menu is extensive, including variations of a traditional English breakfast (the Big One, the English One, the Vegetarian One, the Vegan One), an avocado and egg 'slam', and 'Toast the People!' where customers eat as much fresh baked sourdough as they like (or can) within an hour.

Flour to The People! has a second site in Camberwell.

Local Hero

640 Fulham Rd
SW6 5RT

localherocoffee.co.uk

Local Hero opened in 2004 with the aim of creating a warm and inviting joint in the heart of Fulham's residential neighbourhood, where customers could drink great coffee and munch on brunch and toasties.

Mornings are busy, starting with early commuters getting their daily dose of take-away coffees, and regular locals staying for something to eat. Breakfasts are stunning and delicious, with eggs (Clarence Court) and avocado taking centre stage. Menu favourites include stacked courgette fritters and the thick brioche French toast topped with fresh berries and mascarpone. The team also ensures they create flavourful dishes that are gluten free, vegetarian or vegan.

With white walls and wooden tables, Local Hero boasts a relaxing pergola garden at the back of the café where customers can enjoy long sunny mornings.

Local Hero have another location on Thames Street in Kingston (not dog friendly).

Brooks & Gao

28 Streatham High Rd
SW16 1EX

Brooks & Gao is a Streatham coffee house, showcasing daily fresh food with a Spanish, Italian and French influence.

Combining a modern London feel and a classic European café décor, bare brick walls and wooden panel tables make for an effortlessly laid-back morning setting. The café is kitted out with pavement tables, which are ideal for people watching while sipping on a freshly squeezed juice or a coffee (Coleman Coffee). Located on the high street, the café sees a lot of familiar faces, who quickly become first-name basis regulars.

Brooks & Gao value the simplicity of good produce and quality ingredients that may only need a touch of oil and salt. Trend-led breakfasts are a no-no here, but you're quick to forget about them with dishes such as the ham and eggs, which consists of Trentino smoked speck, two Burford brown eggs (Clarence Court) and salsa verde – a dish inspired by Amsterdam.

Cut the Mustard

68 Moyser Rd
SW16 6SQ

cutthemustardcafe.com

Cut the Mustard is a favourite amongst Tooting and Streatham locals, best known for seasonal brunches, sourdough bread and freshly roasted coffee sourced from a roastery nearby.

Distressed wood is used for flooring and furniture, with food-related items like cookbooks and copper pans sitting on the hanging shelves by the large front windows. You can people watch on the pavement tables outside, if you're not too busy scanning their perfect sourdough (baked in house) displayed on vintage wooden crates – be sure to take a loaf home.

The café menu is considerate, offering alternatives to make breakfast options vegetarian or vegan. Dishes are also thoughtful, changing constantly to use the best of seasonal ingredients. Friendly staff serve up breakfast items such as the 'Obligatory Granola' and variations of their buttermilk pancakes. Poached eggs sit on top of well-constructed dishes like the nduja toast, with nduja (a spicy pork and pepper paste), goats' cheese, butter beans and herbs on sourdough.

Salon

18 Market Row
SW9 8LD

salonbrixton.co.uk

SAT
SUN

Tucked inside Brixton's Market Row, Salon offers seasonal British food in a relaxed environment. Starting as a pop-up in 2012, an increasing demand for their innovative food led the team to continuously do more events until they opened up their permanent Brixton site, in what was originally a cheese shop with a large store room upstairs – now their dining room.

The team work with small suppliers, and as well as being guided by seasons, they are also driven by locality. Salon are inspired by what's around them, allowing them to have a sense of place, but also be influenced by different cultures and flavours. Nicholas Balfe, Salon's Chef Patron, along with the rest of the team, forage frequently from Brockwell Park on their way to work.

Morning highlights include their shakshuka, which evolves depending on which ingredients are in season, as well as the sriracha royale (house-smoked salmon, rye soda bread, poached duck egg, greens and sriracha chilli hollandaise) and tomato bruschetta during summer months. Brunch is best served with one of their special fermented chilli Bloody Marys with cardamom and vodka.

174

BREAKFAST LONDON

Shakshuka

SERVES 1

Sauce (The sauce makes
2 litres, enough for
about 10 servings)
5 shallots
½ head of garlic
10g fresh thyme
a splash of olive oil
2.5kg tomatoes, peeled
  and chopped
pinch of paprika
5g dried chilli flakes
½ fresh red chilli
50ml pickled chilli brine
  (or a pinch of sugar
  and a dash of vinegar)

To serve (per dish)
2 eggs or 1 duck egg
a handful of feta, crumbled
1 tsp pickled chilli (Salon
  pickles theirs in a brine made
  from 1 part water, 1 part
  sugar, 1 part vinegar)
a pinch of sumac
a handful of fresh herbs
salt and pepper
a couple of slices of flatbread,
  pita or another bread

Shakshuka is a mouth-watering Middle Eastern dish, with eggs baked in a rich tomato sauce and topped with feta amongst other elements. On Salon's menu, the dish's ingredients change with the seasons, however this version can be made all year round. Be sure to serve with plenty of bread for dipping and plate cleaning.

First make the sauce. Finely chop the shallots, garlic and thyme and fry together in a large heavy-based pan with olive oil and salt until the shallots start to break down and go sticky. Add the chopped tomatoes, paprika, chilli flakes, fresh chilli pricked with sharp knife, plus pickled chilli brine for some sweetness and sharpness (alternatively add a pinch of sugar and dash of vinegar). Cook this very gently over a low heat for 2 hours, stirring regularly, until it is reduced by one fifth. Then take off the heat and cool. The sauce can be kept for 3 days in the fridge or frozen and is also good as a base for a spiced pasta dish.

To serve, heat one small frying pan, over a medium-high heat, add a ladle of the tomato sauce mixture and leave until the sauce starts to bubble. Then add 2 eggs per person, cover with a lid and leave over a medium heat for 6–10 minutes until the eggs are done to your liking. Then remove from the heat, top with feta cheese, pickled chilli, sumac, fresh herbs and salt and pepper. Serve with flatbreads, pita or toast.

Flotsam & Jetsam

4 Bellevue Parade
SW17 7EQ

flotsamandjetsamcafe.co.uk

A stone's throw from Wandsworth Common, Flotsam and Jetsam is almost constantly bustling with friendly staff, local residents and those from further afield who know that the breakfast here is worth the travel.

The café is bright and breezy, with whitewashed walls, mermaid green countertops and hanging planters that have made their way from New Zealand. The space adapts well with the seasons – cosy in the winter months, and with a sun-soaked outdoor area and bi-folding windows that are opened right out in the summer.

Dishes use seasonal, fresh and natural ingredients, made in-house where possible (like their coconut yoghurt and homemade granola), and cater for dairy-free, gluten-free and vegans. The banana bread with cinnamon butter is a popular staple (a recipe developed by co-founder Hana's mum), and the huevos rancheros and smashed avocado with feta and pickled chillies are also customer favourites.

Order an Allpress coffee to go alongside your breakfast, or a colourful latte such as the Butterfly (blue matcha, passionfruit and almond), or even a decadent hot chocolate made with melted Belgian dark chocolate.

Regency Café

17–19 Regency St
SW1P 4BY

regencycafe.co.uk

Regency Café is arguably London's most famous greasy spoon café, having been voted as one of the top places to eat in town multiple times. A good British café with a menu to match, it's an ideal spot to get your fry up fix.

The site is eye-catching, with an art deco exterior utilising black tiling around large windows, and a neon café sign – just so you really can't miss it. The authentic décor takes you back to the post-war period, with ceramic white tiles that are original from their opening in 1946. Walls are adorned with photographs, including snaps of Tottenham Hotspur footballers and stills from the movie *Layer Cake*, which featured the café (Regency Café has appeared in a handful of TV shows, movies, adverts and even a *Vogue* shoot).

Be sure to order at the counter before you take a seat, and then wait for the friendly staff to bellow your order when it's ready for you to collect. Plates are a generous sea of beans, bacon, fried eggs, chips, sausages, black pudding and bubble and squeak, with toast and butter on the side and all the condiments you need on the tables. Hearty and delicious, the food here is fantastic value.

Regency Café is cash only.

Senzala Creperie

41-42 Brixton Village Market SW9 8PS

senzalacreperie.co.uk

In the heart of Brixton Village Market, you'll find Senzala – a crêperie, bar and café specialising in savoury and sweet crêpes, as well as buckwheat galettes.

The menu challenges the ideas of a traditional crêpe, packed with options including gluten-free and vegan selections that are both delicious and affordable. The café's owners are Brazilian, and the approach throughout Senzala is 'French with a Brazilian flair', although they also draw on a variety of global influences. This is reflected in popular menu staples like the el egg ranchero (with chorizo, egg, beans, jalapeños and guacamole), and the salmon panache (with smoked salmon, asparagus, egg and crème fraîche), as well as new specials and an abundance of savoury and sweet extras.

Senzala's Brazilian roots can also be appreciated throughout the space, from the restaurant's décor to the music, as well as the buzz of a bustling bistro full of energy. And for avid people watchers, Senzala possesses one of the market's best views.

Senzala has a vegan sister restaurant, Pipoca, focusing on vegan crêpes and galettes on Brixton Road.

178

Tried & True

279 Upper Richmond Rd SW15 6SP

triedandtruecafe.co.uk

If you live in Putney, Tried & True is that place where the barista knows your name and daily order, and you're likely to bump into other friendly faces from your neighbourhood enjoying their coffee or morning meal.

The café is spacious with splashes of colour highlighting the calm décor of tile and oak, and generous banquet seating that means parties of any size can be seated together. Throughout the summer months the sun-drenched courtyard is a popular spot to dine, as are the pavement tables where you can sip a flat white as you watch the world move.

Tried & True concentrate on two things: food and coffee. The breakfast menu's stand out dish is the award-winning BBQ pulled pork benedict – spice rubbed fifteen-hour roasted pork shoulder, tossed in hickory hoisin sauce, served on homemade jalapeño cheddar cornbread and topped with two poached eggs, chilli butter and spring onions. The skillet hash with chorizo picante is also worth an order.

Café Fleur

198 St Ann's Hill
SW18 2RT

cafefleurwandsworth.com

Café Fleur is the cosy neighbourhood café you'd want down the road. Many customers comment that it's like being in their own living room, since the café interior has a homely vibe. Lucy, the owner, has collected furnishings and fixtures over the years from her childhood home, secondhand shops, or had them handmade by local carpenters.

Lucy decided to keep the name of what was once an old greasy spoon and gave the spot a new lease of life. From vegan plates to a meat feast, their menu caters to all, and you can still find a full English on the menu, as well as a full vegan. Plates are created with fresh, local ingredients and homemade where possible. Any dish with Chef Oscar's homemade chilli sauce is a winner, and favourites include chilli avocado on organic sourdough and the 'Fleur Bubble', Lucy's take on bubble and squeak. Choose from fresh juices, speciality coffee (Volcano Coffee Works) and brunch cocktails to have alongside your morning meal.

Ground Coffee Society

79 Lower Richmond Rd SW15 1ET

groundcoffeesociety.com

Ground Coffee Society is an independently owned speciality coffee bar and roastery, serving up breakfasts and coffees to Putney locals and south-west London residents. Bustling even on weekdays, weekends see queues for take-away coffees and pastries, and groups hovering to grab the next available table.

Owners and founders Dave and Tracey Dickinson have built a solid reputation for delivering one of the most loved coffee shops in the area, teaming up with celebrity couple Ronan and Storm Keating to expand their coffee offering further. Ground Coffee Society has roasted and served their own coffee since 2009 – their roastery in Bicester packs over 1200kg of coffee every week, which gets sent out to customers and is also available to purchase through their website.

The front section of the café is dedicated to take-aways, with attractive brick walls, hanging pendant lamps and baked goods temptingly on display. Down a few steps are wooden tables with metal chairs for those eating in, and beyond this sits a courtyard with fairy lights and a retractable roof for sunnier days.

'Caveman' is the café's house blend on offer daily, ready to be poured into a flat white or sold in bags. Breakfast is both attractive and delicious, featuring breakfast burritos, quinoa power pots and the highly recommended blueberry pancakes – American-style buttermilk pancakes with bacon, blueberry compote and mascarpone.

Dogs are welcome outside and in the take-away area at the front of the café, but are not allowed in the seating area.

Farm Girl

9 Park Walk
SW10 0AJ

thefarmgirl.co.uk

Farm Girl presents a healthy approach to Australian café culture, offering a bright and buzzing atmosphere in which to enjoy wholesome food and speciality coffee (The Roasting Party). The innovative menu features items such as acai smoothie bowls, coconut bacon and superfood lattes, as well as brunch staples berry pancakes and the house granola, which have a permanent place on the morning menu. Accompanying the brunch selection, there is a daily assortment of pastries and gluten-free cakes on offer.

The back of the Chelsea restaurant is a focal point, with bulb-framed pink arches surrounding an airy and plant-filled skylight, which creates a perfect setting for those breakfast snaps. The restaurant is spacious, with the capacity to seat eighty guests and the small sun-drenched terrace fitting a further ten diners.

Farm Girl has other locations in Notting Hill and Carnaby Street.

Chairs & Coffee

512 Fulham Rd
SW6 5NJ

chairsandcoffee.co.uk

Not only do they make banana bread that's become well known around the neighbourhood, but they roast their own coffee too, so Chairs & Coffee ticks a lot of boxes. The menu is a combination of the owners Simone Guerini Rocco and Roberto d'Alessandro's experiences, as well as current trends. The avocado on sourdough is the most popular dish, so they regularly change the dressing and toppings in order to give customers a taste of something new without taking away the bestseller. Another customer favourite is the scrambled eggs on sourdough with taleggio cheese, sautéed mushrooms, grilled chorizo and a side of avocado.

True to their name, chairs hang from the café's ceiling. The style is vintage, and the curated background music adds to the relaxed weekday mood or bustling weekend vibe. On warmer days, their patio is an ideal place for people watching and sun-soaking.

Chairs & Coffee has a second location in Elephant & Castle, 80 Stone Café, which is now the flagship store of their coffee roasting company.

Burnt Toast Café

88 Brixton Village Market
SW9 8PS

With breakfast options on every corner of Brixton Market, Burnt Toast Café ensures it stands out. Their exterior isn't fancy – darkly painted with graffiti – and tables are out in front of their unit (their kitchen is inside) so you're sat in the heart of the market. What sets them apart is their food.

Breakfast is served all day at Burnt Toast Café. The team serve smashing house roasted coffee and bake fantastic bread, pastries and cakes freshly in-house. The photo-worthy breakfasts are full of colour, popping from the deep, white enamel plates they're served on.

Like most places, they change up the menu frequently. However, the crisp yet fluffy buttermilk pancakes are a must-order, with varying toppings like toffee and bacon or caramelised banana with mixed berries. There's plenty of savoury options too, including a few eggs benedict variations, and you can even burn your own toast in the toaster outside before slathering on delicious jams and spreads.

West London is where you'll find the city's established department stores and swanky hotels filled with attentive staff and buffets of morning essentials. Coffees and croissants are consumed whilst swanning through Hyde Park, which comes to life in the summertime, hosting bike rides, rowing boats on the Serpentine and festivals. Further out, the vibrant district of Notting Hill is bursting with cafés. The unique character of this diverse area is shown through its annual carnival and the famous Portobello Market, with popular breakfast spots along and nearby Golborne Road. Strolling by the pubs along the River Thames in Hammersmith and Chiswick after brunch, you might forget you're in London at all.

OPSO • **The Dayrooms Café** • Angie's Little Food Shop • **NAC** • EggBreak • **Granger & Co.** • NOPI • **Over Under Coffee** • Ffiona's • **Mac & Wild** • Truth Café • **The Wolseley** • The Providores and Tapa Room • **Golborne Deli & Bistro** • Pachamama • **Koya** • Snaps + Rye • **Lantana** • High Mood Food • **Berners Tavern** • Urban Pantry • **Jikoni**

OPSO

10 Paddington St
W1U 5QL

opso.co.uk

SAT
SUN

Based in Marylebone, mornings at
OPSO (the ancient Greek word for
'delicacy') fuses traditional Greek
ingredients and tastes with UK breakfast
favourites, such as bacon and eggs.
Baked goods take a central role on the
menu, showcasing freshly baked koulouri
bread (sesame-seed covered milk bread)
as well as tsoureki (a sweet flavoured
brioche), which is served alongside
a decadent chocolate-praline spread.

'I think it's just because we like
baked goods,' says Head Chef Sergej
Nikolajev, matter-of-factly. 'We like
breads. I like to start my day when
I smell freshly baked bread. It makes
sense for me.' In the OPSO kitchen,
the smell of freshly baked bread rolls
in from four o'clock in the morning.

The weekend-only brunch plates
are, fortunately, designed for sharing.
Colourful breakfast options include
photo-worthy pancakes and homemade
granola topped with Greek honey. Their
'Eggs and Chips' – fresh-cooked chips
topped with feta, tomatoes and a duck
egg on top – are also worth ordering.

For accompanying morning drinks,
diners can sip on fresh juices, fruit
smoothies made with Greek yoghurt,

and Ibrik coffee – a traditional Greek coffee – either plain or infused with rosewater. The bar also serves up a selection of cocktails using Greek liqueurs and spirits for those looking for a boozier weekend brunch.

Like their menu, OPSO's interior is a modern blend of elements taken from Greek and British design, combining natural oak panelling with urban steel structures. While there's a bar and dining space upstairs, on the lower-ground floor is 'The Larder', which contains an additional dining area and intimate booths, as well as a view of OPSO's curing chambers and wine fridge. Snuggle indoors during the winter months, or be sure to grab an in-demand table outside when the sun's shining.

The Dayrooms Café

212 Kensington Park Rd
W11 1NR

thedayroomscafe.com

In a sea of Australian-inspired cafés in London, The Dayrooms Café remains memorable. The food – taste, quality and presentation – is the fundamental reason behind this. Taking inspiration from what's new and popular in the breakfast world then adding their own twist to it, the café keeps things simple, but special. Dishes like their salmon and egg stuffed croissant with truffle hollandaise, and the stunning Bircher muesli topped with crème fraîche, lemon curd, berries and mint, are just a couple of the options that'll keep you coming back.

Tucked away on one of the quieter streets of Notting Hill, customers can expect to find an intimate, local neighbourhood café with a modern, minimal and plant-loving interior to match. Pop in for a take-away coffee (Ozone Coffee Roasters) or make some time for a sit down brunch.

The Dayrooms Café has a second location in Holborn, which focuses on take-away breakfast, lunch and coffee.

➡

Angie's Little Food Shop

114 Chiswick High Rd
W4 1PU

angieslittlefoodshop.com

A neighbourhood brunch spot with a loyal following of regulars, Angie's Little Food Shop serves breakfast favourites with a chilled-out vibe.

Angie's background is in fine dining – she trained under Gordon Ramsay for eight years. However, her desire was to create a more relaxed dining experience than the high-end environment she had practiced in, and thus Angie's Little Food Shop was born.

On the menu you'll find a mix of classic breakfast items and noteworthy dishes, including the ever-pleasing scrambled eggs with smoked salmon and the wild mushrooms on toasted brioche. The blueberry hotcakes with espresso mascarpone and a vanilla cinnamon sauce also make a perfect start to any morning. Order with a cold-pressed juice or a coffee sourced from The Roasting Party, based near Winchester.

Mornings are filled with families and social catch-ups, and are especially busy on the weekends. However, the space never feels cramped with its light and airy interior, decorated with South African ceramics (which are also for sale).

NAC

41 North Audley St
W1K 6ZP

naclondon.co.uk

North Audley Cantine, also known as
NAC, seems as if it was created to be
photographed. Inside, the restaurant
has a New York influence, with leather
banquette booth seating and whitewashed
brick walls. Their basement has a 1940s
Hollywood vibe with green velvet seating,
white marble tables, golden brass pendant
lights and blush pink walls. Throw in
their Paris-inspired terrace (perfect for
al fresco brunching), and you could be
tempted to visit just for the décor alone.

The food is just as photogenic.
Ricotta pancakes drenched in dulce
de leche and topped with banana are
a customer favourite, along with the
shakshuka and 'eggs Norwegian'. NAC
takes pride in their cocktails, considering
seasonality for their drinks as much as
their food. Be sure to order their Bloody
Mary, done with a twist of sriracha sauce.
Finish off weekend brunch with a portion
of the milk chocolate cookies for the table
– if you think you can share. Mornings at
NAC are best enjoyed amongst friends,
and are suited for any occasion.

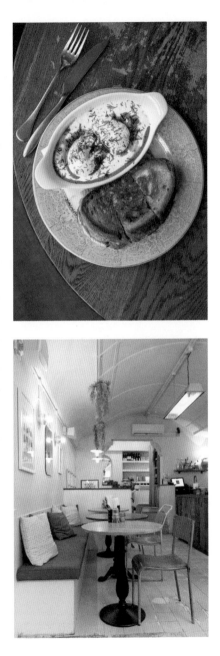

EggBreak

30 Uxbridge St
W8 7TA

eggbreak.com

A relaxed neighbourhood café tucked away on a street in Notting Hill, EggBreak serves spins on classic breakfast dishes using quality produce. Based on LA's EggSlut, EggBreak is an all-day concept centred around – you've guessed it – eggs.

Delicious omelettes, Turkish eggs, Middle Eastern shakshuka and plenty more egg-related plates feature on their menu. Their free-range eggs, supplied by Fenton Farm, can be found on top of smashed avocado or drenched under sriracha hollandaise. Other breakfast options are just as tempting – the drool-inducing cornflake-coated stuffed French toast never fails to win over customers. Pair dishes with coffees (Origins), teas (Canton) or fresh cold-pressed juices.

EggBreak's breakfast items are no stranger to a social feed, which invites out-the-door queues on weekends, especially as they don't take reservations. Weekdays see more regulars, who come in for an early breakfast, a quick meeting or just a coffee whilst reading the paper.

Granger & Co.

175 Westbourne Grove
W11 2SB

grangerandco.com

Granger & Co. brings Sydney-style, all-day dining to London thanks to Australian chef Bill Granger, known for his restaurants Bill's in Sydney.

Embracing the sunny, vibrant, feel-good food that is reflective of the Aussie spirit, Granger & Co. has an easy-going approach to dining with a menu that focuses on fresh flavours and ingredients. It's difficult not to eye up their creamy scrambled eggs, especially with sourdough toast and a side of avocado. However, the restaurant is famous for their fluffy ricotta hotcakes served with banana and honeycomb butter, which is available daily until 5pm. Light, bright and welcoming, the fashionable no-reservations Notting Hill restaurant features a cluster of tables and a bar with counter dining, as well as a few tables outside. Spend mornings here with a newspaper, family members or a small group of friends.

Granger & Co. also has locations in Chelsea, Clerkenwell and King's Cross.

NOPI

ottolenghi.co.uk

'The Ottolenghi Formula', as described by Yotam Ottolenghi, is vegetable heavy. He highlights the herbs, spices, freshness of citrus and the employment of big gestures when it comes to food presentation. Though it has the same emphasis on Middle Eastern flavours found at all Ottolenghi establishments, the menu at NOPI also has Asian elements influenced by Malaysian-born, Sydney-raised previous Head Chef Ramael Scully.

For NOPI, the idea was to take the bold flavours and beautifully plated presentation for which Ottolenghi is so famous and showcase them in a slightly more West End, grown-up version of the other deli-style locations. Originally, NOPI was formed to be a brasserie. 'I don't think it feels like a brasserie,' admits Yotam, 'But it still operates almost the whole day . . . and offers the same range of flavours, which are anywhere from the Middle East to Southeast Asia, and interesting combinations from these parts of the world.'

Recognising that people crave familiar breakfast dishes, eggs feature in the morning menu – but an egg dish at NOPI is no ordinary egg dish.

The shakshuka has all sorts of interesting spices and flavours. Even NOPI's variation of a porridge dish consists of black rice with coconut milk, infused with pandan and topped with banana and mango, embracing the comforting flavours of Asia. The focus is on creating morning dishes that aren't overly spicy or complicated, yet more comforting than menu items that feature later in the day.

Located in Soho, the interior blend of white brick and tile walls, wooden chairs and brass and marble features are stunning. The refined restaurant is an ideal spot for meetings or mornings to impress. At the very least, be sure to order a croissant, and pay a visit to their spectacular loos.

BREAKFAST LONDON

Scrambled Tofu with Mashed Avocado & Tomato Salad

From NOPI

SERVES 6

Mashed avocado
3 ripe avocados
1 tbsp green harissa
½ tsp lime zest
1 tsp lime juice
2 tsp olive oil

Tomato salad
300g datterini tomatoes
60g spring onions, finely
    sliced on an angle
1 tbsp olive oil
1 tbsp lemon juice

Scrambled tofu
2 tbsp olive oil
2 onions, finely sliced (300g)
1½ tbsp rose harissa
700g silken tofu, drained

To serve
6 pieces sourdough (or other
    gluten-free bread), grilled
    or toasted
120g mixed leaves
flaked sea salt and
    black pepper

If you can't get hold of green harissa, some finely chopped green chilli and coriander will brighten up your avocado mash. Try to get the datterini tomatoes in red and yellow, if you can.

Add the avocado, green harissa, lime zest, lime juice, oil and a pinch of salt to a small bowl and mash together until well combined.

Combine the tomatoes with the spring onions, olive oil, lemon juice, a generous pinch of salt and a good grind of pepper.

Place a large frying pan over a medium-high heat and add the oil. Add the onions and fry for 9–10 minutes, stirring frequently until caramelised and soft. Add the rose harissa to the onions and continue to stir for 1 minute, then add the tofu and ¾ teaspoon of salt. Use a masher to break up the tofu so it looks like scrambled eggs and continue to heat for 2 minutes so it's hot. Serve the scrambled tofu on the grilled or toasted sourdough with the avocado, tomato salad and mixed leaves alongside.

Over Under Coffee

181A Earls Court Rd
SW5 9RB

overundercoffee.com

There aren't a whole lot of places around Earl's Court that aren't part of a high street chain. But right across the road from Earl's Court Underground Station, you'll find Over Under Coffee, a cosy hole-in-the-wall café. Stripped back to basics with a minimalist feel, it's not uncommon for coffee queues to extend out the door from the tiny space, and snapping up a table at peak time provokes a celebratory air punch.

With expert baristas who care about your name and order, the team work in close partnership with their roaster, Brixton's Assembly Coffee, when sourcing their beans – so you can rely on a consistently excellent cup. Breakfast dishes are simple yet satisfying, including classics such as avocado toast and various porridges and pastries, as well as more uncommon options like their fig toast.

Mornings are booming from 6:30am with disco music and staff banter, making it the ideal stop for early risers, as well as those looking for a take-away or quick breakfast.

Over Under Coffee has a second location in Ham Yard, Soho.

Ffiona's

51 Kensington Church St
W8 4BA

ffionas.com

Ffiona's is a vibrant British restaurant just off Kensington High Street, with a surprisingly unassuming shopfront. However, it's hard to ignore somewhere claiming to have London's 'best brunch' on blackboards perched outside and on their website – a statement supported by many Londoners and tourists alike. Even actress Renée Zellweger is said to be a fan.

Although an intimate space, the restaurant's décor has character, with wooden furniture and attractive wallpaper of blue and white houses. Ffiona herself is a lively presence within the restaurant with attention to detail and a friendly word for all of her customers.

At breakfast, the kitchen serves up a killer French toast topped with berries and sprinkled with icing sugar (or opt for sausage and eggs instead), a divine sweet potato, chorizo and red chilli hash topped with two eggs, and various versions of eggs benedict, amongst other mouth-watering menu options and side dishes. Devour with a coffee, fresh juice or a brunch cocktail.

Mac & Wild

65 Great Titchfield St
W1W 7PS

macandwild.com

Weekend-only brunch at Mac & Wild takes your mind and taste buds on a trip to the Highlands. The team specialises in Scottish produce, working hard to showcase the very best that Scotland has to offer to Londoners.

Mac & Wild began their journey as the Scottish street food sensation Wild Game Co., and their menu maintains a heavy meat focus. The brunch menu features classics served with a Scottish twist, such as their dirty Scottish breakfast bap, eggs Ruaridh, and the crushed avocado on sourdough toast – with a haggis topping.

The bi-level restaurant is decked out with Scottish personality and a Scandi vibe, including images from their game suppliers Ardgay Game and tables created from a tree hit by lightning on a co-founder's farm.

The restaurant also offers a popular bottomless brunch option, where guests can choose from unlimited Bloody Marys, Bloody Scotsmans (whisky), Bloody Botanists (gin) as well as prosecco, bucks fizz and buckie royales.

Mac & Wild has a second location on Devonshire Square.

Truth Café

34 Fulham Palace Rd
W6 9PH

truthcafe.co.uk

The only thing you really need to know about Truth Café is that their breakfast is excellent. The Hammersmith spot is mainly known for their drool-inducing pancake stacks, with flavoursome toppings that include apple, salted caramel and pretzels, as well as banana, Nutella and espresso mascarpone. The Mexican eggs benedict and the sweet potato waffles (gluten-free) with bacon, halloumi or smoked salmon are also worth telling your friends about.

Although fond of adding fresh trimmings to traditional dishes, classics such as omelettes, porridge and a full English also appear on the menu. Smoothies and juices are made fresh to order, while the coffee is supplied by the fantastic Allpress.

Truth Café is bustling every morning, serving take-away coffees and pastries to commuters, and hosting quick breakfasts and work meetings for those nearby. The space is also ideal for catch-ups and hangover fixes, any day of the week.

The Wolseley

<u>160 Piccadilly</u>
<u>W1J 9EB</u>

thewolseley.com

The Wolseley has a way of making every morning feel like a special occasion. The iconic building in Piccadilly was originally built as a prestigious car showroom in 1921, and The Wolseley opened its doors as a 'Grand Café' in 2003, with a striking interior effortlessly combining British heritage with European grandeur.

Those venturing for breakfast are greeted by welcoming staff, along with a table of inviting viennoiserie made on the premises. The morning menu is extensive, including British classics like devilled kidneys with crispy bacon, grilled kipper with mustard butter and 'The English' – their traditional full English breakfast. However, the must-order dish is the modest eggs benedict, with pillow-like English muffins, perfectly poached eggs and a creamy hollandaise sauce. The Wolseley's indulgent stack of pancakes is also a head-turner, topped with either bacon or berries, and arrives with a pourer for you to douse your dish with tremendously generous helpings of syrup.

The Providores and Tapa Room

109 Marylebone High St W1U 4RX

theprovidores.co.uk

The first thing you need to know about The Providores and Tapa Room is that they are in fact two separate sections of the same restaurant: the Providores on the first floor acts as the more formal dining room, whereas the Tapa Room – our breakfast focus – is the relaxed all-day café, coffee shop and wine bar on the ground level. Both rooms serve fusion dishes that utilise internationally sourced ingredients and techniques.

The second point, and arguably the most important one, can be explained with just two simple words: Turkish eggs. Peter Gordon's simple masterpiece of two poached eggs, whipped yoghurt and hot Aleppo chilli butter is paired with a choice of toasted sourdough or seeded granary, and has remained both a menu staple and customer favourite since day one.

Order with a coffee, which is the restaurant's own exclusive coffee blend from Volcano Coffee Works, and a Crosstown doughnut to take home.

Golborne Deli & Bistro

100 Golborne Rd
W10 5PS

golbornedeli.com

Locals make the daily breakfast pilgrimage to Golborne Deli & Bistro for a good reason. An unpretentious setting with hearty food, it's a convenient spot to read the morning paper with a coffee (Butterworth & Sons), catch up over an eggs benedict, or watch the world go by on the outside terrace.

Pictures and photographs from local artists adorn the walls, while the assortment of tables and chairs, both old and new, were brought in to give character and a 1980s vibe to the space. The furniture changes regularly to keep things exciting, sourced from surrounding shops and stalls on Golborne Road.

Above all, Golborne Deli & Bistro are considerate. The staff are welcoming, so much so that they gift panettones to regulars every Christmas. The menu also reflects this, with options for vegans, raw eaters, dairy-free and gluten-free customers. Popular breakfast choices include the hearty deli breakfast and vegan breakfast.

212

Pachamama

18 Thayer St
W1U 3JY

pachamamalondon.com

SAT
SUN

When you think of Pachamama's weekend-only brunch, you think of waffles.

Freshly made to order, customers have a choice between sweet potato or quinoa waffles, that are then adorned with toppings and transformed into individual dishes. The sweet variations include the decadently rich Peruvian chocolate with toasted quinoa ice cream and cacao crumb, and savoury embraces the colourful beetroot-cured smoked salmon, avocado and poached egg option. Sat on pastel-coloured plates, the dishes are strikingly photogenic if you manage to capture a picture without tucking in instantaneously. Ordering multiple dishes to share (or to keep to yourself) is highly recommended.

For those wanting something different, the brunch menu contains ceviche and other Peruvian-inspired specials. Using Peru's traditional recipes as a focal point, the kitchen applies an array of techniques and flavours to create the variety of delicious dishes they offer, all of which are perfectly washed down with a pisco sour or two. Brunch cocktails are whipped up behind the elongated bar named 'Papa's Bar' in a bright neon light, while dishes are collected from a kitchen window under the sign 'Mama's Kitchen'.

Pachamama has a second location – Pachamama East – in Shoreditch, and a sister restaurant called Chicama in Chelsea.

➡

Koya

50 Frith St
W1D 4SQ

koya.co.uk

For udon-lovers, this Soho spot deserves a place at the top of your list. Koya specialises in udon and makes thick, chewy noodles in house every day, serving them in various ways along with seasonal specials. Beyond their signature neon sign of a red house, you'll find long wooden counters with an open kitchen, where you can witness the talented chefs in action.

The breakfast menu is made up of udon, rice and rice porridge dishes, created to reflect locality and seasonality. The classic Japanese breakfast, which consists of grilled fish with rice and miso soup, is a chef favourite. Other popular items are their unique take on kedgeree and the English breakfast (fried egg, bacon and shiitake mushrooms), served in either a bowl of udon and homemade fish-based dashi (vegan dashi is also available), or with rice porridge. Vegetables are from Namayasai, a farm in Lewes growing Japanese vegetables, and are picked and delivered to Koya on the same day, to make sure they are as good as it gets.

Koya has a second location in Bloomberg Arcade, however this branch does not serve breakfast.

Snaps + Rye

93 Golborne Rd
W10 5NL

snapsandrye.com

Snaps + Rye is a modern Nordic
restaurant on the eclectic Golborne
Road. A long-term dream of a husband
and wife partnership, the Danish and
English duo serve fresh and clean
flavours from seasonal ingredients,
including a lot of fish – cured, smoked,
pickled and fresh. Their famous and
addictive kedgeree is packed full of
smoked haddock and cured salmon.

    The morning menu, served Tuesday
to Sunday, is comprised of Danish
delights such as freshly baked pastries
and the classic smørrebrød – open
sandwiches on their homemade rye
bread with breakfast options of cured
salmon, avocado or egg. The gull Danish
(rye rarebit, hogs pudding, smoked
bacon, spinach, tomatoes) is also
worth a mention, as well as the popular
scrambled eggs with cured var salmon and
homemade Danish rye bread. Plates are
best washed down with a Danish Bloody
Viking cocktail, featuring their homemade
dill snaps, or a liquorice latte.

➡

216

Lantana

13 Charlotte Pl
W1T 1SN

lantanacafe.co.uk

Australia is deservedly famous for its café culture and Lantana thinks of itself as 'a little bit of Australia in London'. You can expect delicious breakfast and brunch dishes with a multicultural twist, quality coffee and warm customer service. Coffee is roasted by Alchemy Roastery, who create a bespoke blend for Lantana, which they develop together throughout the year as the seasons change. For food, Lantana's bestseller is the corn fritters, stacked with streaky bacon, fresh spinach, roast tomatoes, smashed avocado and lemon crème fraîche, best ordered with an added poached egg and chilli jam.

With a relaxed vibe but vibrant energy, breakfast service is their busiest with customers using the café for meetings, social get-togethers and as a work space. In the summer, Lantana's front windows open and customers flock to the outside tables on the pedestrianised street. Next door to the dine-in café, Lantana have a small take-away shop serving freshly baked goods, breakfast treats, take-away coffee and fresh juices.

Lantana also has sites in Shoreditch and London Bridge.

High Mood Food

25 Duke St
W1U 1LD

highmoodfood.com

You might not pay much attention to your gut health, but High Mood Food does. Founded by Ursel Barnes and Joey O'Hare, the café combines Ursel's vast knowledge of holistic wellbeing with Joey's culinary expertise.

An oasis off Oxford Street, High is known for its pink Himalayan salt brick counter, and large split citrine crystals sit in the store to contain the space's good energy. The central spot sees mostly take-away trade, although they have window seats at the front of the store, as well as a small seating area at the rear.

With a seasonal and veg-centric breakfast menu, dishes are enhanced with the complex flavours and live bacteria of fermented foods. On weekday mornings, customers can build their own breakfast bowl, including the must-try black barley and white miso porridge. Those with more time can experience options like the poached eggs and avocado on sourdough, topped with seeds and 'living hot sauce' – a fermented chilli dressing with hints of garlic and ginger, kept raw so live bacteria from fermentation remains intact.

High's more elaborate weekend brunch menu features gut healthy twists

on breakfast classics, with warm toasted banana bread, organic vanilla labneh and tahini, and open sandwiches on their 'Happy Tummy' bread – made with organic teff flour and ground almonds, it is naturally gluten-free and high in prebiotic fibre.

High Mood Food has a second location in Old Spitalfields Market.

Berners Tavern

10 Berners St
W1T 3NP

editionhotels.com

Chef and restaurateur Jason Atherton launched Berners Tavern in 2013 within The London EDITION hotel, but it is far from another hotel restaurant. On Berners Street in Fitzrovia, it seats 140 and remains one of London's ultimate spots to impress.

Set within a sophisticated grand dining room, the restaurant presents a seamless fusion of modern and period design. Large bronze chandeliers, inspired by NYC's Grand Central Station, hang from the ceilings, while the room is adorned with a curated blend of photographic portraits, landscapes and still life. An ideal spot for special meetings or significant occasions, Berners Tavern also offers an intimate private dining room that seats up to fourteen, available for morning gatherings.

The menu is filled with contemporary British dishes, and is described by Jason as 'simple yet elegant, using the best of British ingredients and change of seasons.' Options are varied to cover all tastes, from continental breakfasts, to cooked dishes featuring heritage-breed eggs. Smoothies are dairy-free, with optional health shots and boosters to start your morning.

Urban Pantry

15 Devonshire Rd
W4 2EU

urby-p.com

There's something about Urban Pantry, an Antipodean-style café in Chiswick, that quickly puts you at ease. Customers swiftly become friends of the café, and regulars can often be found catching up with staff.

Wanting to transport people to the chilled-out vibes of Australia and New Zealand, Urban Pantry is decorated in a similar style to a Sydney beachside café, with whitewashed wood panels on the walls, an outdoor terrace and a large window at the front of the store that fully opens out to let sun stream inside. The easy-going venue is perfect for catching up with Mum or reading the paper.

Menu items change monthly to keep things interesting, with a handful of customer favourites remaining as staples. Specials also change every fortnight, highlights of which include quinoa and vanilla pancakes with poached Yorkshire rhubarb and whipped vanilla yoghurt, and traditional Venezuelan cachapas, which are a kind of sweetcorn pancake with melted cheddar and tomato salsa. Their coffee is also special – the team have worked with their friends Capital Coffee Roastery, a family run business, to create the Urban Pantry House Blend.

➡

220

Jikoni

19–21 Blandford St
W1U 3DH

jikonilondon.com

A cosy neighbourhood restaurant in Marylebone, dining at Jikoni feels like you're visiting someone's home, both through the personal décor and the food. The dishes are based on founder Ravinder Bhogal's heritage – East African, Indian and Persian – as well as being inspired by her travels. Their kitchen style is to cook like cooks, not chefs, combining instinct and intuition with seasonal ingredients.

The weekend-only brunches are globally influenced, mentally transporting diners with each and every bite. The piña colada pancakes are a must-try customer favourite, even for savoury lovers – divine coconut pancakes, caramelised pineapple and rum and coconut ice cream. Other highlights include the cornbread with spicy creamed corn and fried egg, and the tamarind glazed bacon with fenugreek waffles. The tender bacon is spice cured, slow-cooked overnight, then cut into thick slabs and crisped up on the plancha.

Thriving city hotspots meet residential bliss in north-west London. Best known is Camden Market with its renowned punk past, now showcasing a variety of independent stores and food traders, including specialised breakfast options. In next-door Kentish Town, fresh ideas and urban enterprises are increasingly being brought to life. Nearby, Primrose Hill in Regent's Park is considered a top destination to experience one of the greatest views over the city. Hampstead Heath's luscious greenery also invites cyclists and strollers to escape the everyday bustle of London life, and is best done with a tea or smoothie in hand.

Ginger & White • Café
Loren • Lazy Hunter • The
Fields Beneath • Mario's
Café • Greenberry Café •
LLS Café • Parlour • La
Crêperie de Hampstead •
Leyas • The Coffee Jar

Ginger & White

4A–5A Perrin's Court
NW3 1QS

gingerandwhite.com

When three friends started Ginger & White in 2009, they had a few aims in mind. They had babies, so they wanted the café to be child-friendly. They also wanted to fill the gap they'd discovered in the availability of good coffee in the outer suburbs of London, and they'd realised that the only decent breakfasts around were at greasy spoons or hotels. As a result, Ginger & White brings the Antipodean celebration of espresso coffee and breakfast to Hampstead.

The café emulates a homely environment, with a communal table and a desire to make everyone feel comfortable, whether they're on their own, in a group or with children. Positioned on a side street in the leafy suburb, it's ideal for dog and pram walkers alike, especially with plenty of seats outside the café.

The small kitchen serves familiar dishes such as boiled eggs and soldiers, bacon butties and their own baked beans. Their hot chocolate is said to be 'legendary', made with British producer Montezuma's flakes and Northiam Dairy milk.

Ginger & White has a second location in Belsize Park.

Café Loren

Unit 5-6 The Stables Market
Chalk Farm Rd
NW1 8AH

cafeloren.co.uk

Café Loren's all-day menu is centred around their favourite dish: shakshuka – the traditional Middle Eastern baked egg breakfast dish. The team serves ten different types of shakshuka, from the traditional to their unique interpretations of the dish, including orange, white and green varieties with different sauce bases, and even a vegan version. They also create a seasonal version that changes monthly, celebrating the fresh vegetables available. All shakshuka dishes are served with a side of fresh homemade bread (gluten-free bread also available).

The popular homeshuka is their granny's recipe and consists of two poached eggs, roasted bell peppers, onions, garlic and tomatoes on a bed of hummus topped with tahini. The Balkan shakshuka is also a customer favourite, with the addition of feta cheese, basil and parsley. Aside from shakshuka, Café Loren serves rainbow bagels and vegan brownies, as well as Monmouth coffee and fresh fruit smoothies.

Located in the entrance of Camden Market, the café looks out over a cobbled courtyard, with outdoor seating for customers. Inside is cosy, with antique furniture and modern lighting.

Lazy Hunter

117 Kentish Town Rd
NW1 8PB

lazyhunter.co.uk

Lazy Hunter serves most of their breakfasts in skillets, which not only results in mouth-watering effects and photos being snapped before hungry breakfast and brunch-goers tuck into their meal, but it can make many nostalgic, with their thoughts drifting far from London.

To Lazy Hunter's owners, the pans represent camping trips and evoke memories of what they cooked on the fire whilst in the countryside. 'What is easy, what is delicious, what reminds you of the countryside,' reminisces Joana, referencing the nostalgic dishes served at the restaurant. Joana is one of the four owners of this family business – the others being her sister, brother-in-law and his brother. She describes her memories of throwing together ingredients like potatoes, spinach, mushrooms and onions, all topped with cheese, into a heavy pan on a fire when she used to go camping.

Similar dishes with varying elements are found on the menu, such as the 'full Hunter's' breakfast, the restaurant's own version of a full English. You'll also find options less common on a campsite but equally as delicious, like the oven-baked pancakes and a juicy breakfast burger.

Portions are generous, and perfectly accompanied by brunch cocktails, a cup of raspberry jam tea or even a chocolate cookie served with milk.

Lazy Hunter's sister restaurant, Melange in Crouch End, is also worth a visit for breakfast or brunch.

The Fields Beneath

52A Prince of Wales Rd
NW5 3LN

thefieldsbeneath.com

The Fields Beneath is a hub for locals in transit, set in a residential area beside Kentish Town West Station – one of the rare London train stations not on a high street. You won't be able to miss them as a yellow road sign on the footpath diverts you right to the café – if you haven't smelt the coffee and baked goods already.

The café care about the customers, the offering and the area. From a sign hung above the counter, you'll learn that the café was named after *The Fields Beneath* written by Gillian Tindall, a book about the history of Kentish Town. There's also a wall adorned with local flyers and adverts, highlighting the central role it plays within the community.

The team started with a coffee cart, and through their journey have become an all-vegan café focusing on tasty food and coffee with a mission of normalising veganism. Mornings are high-energy and intimate; they provide a big welcome and a mini oasis away from everyday life, delighting for a few minutes before sending you out into your day. There are a handful of tables inside, as well as outdoor seating under the railway arch.

Breakfast options are limited but incredibly well done, with highlights including their breakfast muffin packed full with tofu 'egg', hash brown and smoky tomato sauce amongst other elements, as well as hard-to-beat sweet and savoury-stuffed croissants that fly out of the store daily.

The Fields Beneath make the most of the small space with rustic exposed brick, plants and a mirror ball that takes centre stage on sunny days.

Mario's Café

6 Kelly St
NW1 8PH

marioscafe.com

Mario's Café is considered an institution in Kentish Town. Small and unassuming, the café is more than the area's go-to greasy spoon – it's a treasured part of the local community. Saint Etienne even dedicated a song ('Mario's Café') to it, and Ronald Denning made a documentary about the café.

It's Mario himself who makes the place come alive, warmly greeting and serving both regulars and visitors, and creating an environment where even if you visit alone, it never really feels like it.

Thoughtfulness is evident throughout the café, from the food to the walls decorated with exhibiting artists, and even seen in the heart-warming story about the family-run café dating back to 1958 on their website.

The extremely reasonably priced menu is a mix of British and Italian staples, and breakfast is all about the fry up with optional extras, including the traditional beans, hash browns, black pudding and homemade chips. There are also lighter choices available like granola with yoghurt or scrambled eggs with smoked salmon on ciabatta. Grab a seat outside and gaze at the colourful terraced cottages along Kelly Street.

Greenberry Café

101 Regent's Park Rd
NW1 8UR

greenberrycafe.co.uk

The lively atmosphere, friendly staff and flexible all-day menus quickly established Greenberry Café as a prime breakfast and meeting spot for Primrose Hill locals.

On the site of old Russian tea rooms, the café is bright – so ideal for those snapping a picture of their good-looking brekkie. Mirrors sit below black and white photographs of local artists, writers, broadcasters and musicians with another well lit bare brick area towards the back of the café. Jazz and blues are the soundtrack to your morning meals here.

Greenberry's breakfast and brunch menus are proud globetrotters. The Middle Eastern-inspired shakshuka sits alongside an English breakfast, a vegetarian breakfast and the Anglo-Indian dish kedgeree with poached eggs. Other favourites include the eggs royale, and the avocado on sourdough with tomato, spring onion and coriander salsa.

The café works with quality suppliers, including Climpson & Sons for coffee (using their Baron blend), old breed Burford Brown eggs from Clarence Court, smoked salmon from H. Forman & Son, and bacon and sausages by Dingley Dell.

LLS Café

95–97 Heath St
NW3 6SS

llscafe.com

LLS café launched with the idea that healthy eating shouldn't mean compromising on taste, textures and flavours. The café focuses on healthy food, a warm atmosphere and quirky menu, with a desire to educate people on the beauty of eating more plants, organically grown and without sugars.

Although LLS is not a vegan café, they encourage customers to eat and drink less animal products with a mantra of 'eat no evil'. The menu is based round a large array of plant-only foods while keeping their offering wide and unjudgemental. Run by two sisters who re-educated their mother on the importance of diet when she was diagnosed with type 2 diabetes, they realised others needed to know how much they could enjoy while cutting out potentially harmful foods.

Their menu is an all-day affair, with favourites such as taktouka (a Moroccan shakshuka), which is their mother's own recipe. The glorious gluten-free LLS pancakes has also made its way around social media feeds.

LLS has two other locations in Waterloo and Paddington.

236

Parlour

5 Regent St
NW10 5LG

parlourkensal.com

Parlour is synonymous with their
'(No Subs) Full Parlour Breakfast',
which has been widely regarded as – at
the very least – one of London's best
full English breakfasts. And if you don't
agree, it may be because you've not
yet laid your eyes on it.

The round, pan-like plate is filled
with everything you'd expect. Fried
Clarence Court eggs are nestled next to
smoked streaky bacon, and Cumberland
sausages from Barrett's Butchers in
Belsize sit alongside homemade hash
browns. Right in the middle of the pan,
however, sits a glass jar of Heinz baked
beans. 'I haven't managed to perfect the
recipe [for homemade beans] yet,' says
Jesse Dunford Wood, Parlour's owner
and head chef, who takes pride in the
high quality of the food made in-house
and hand-picks excellent suppliers. The
dish is served daily until 4:30pm, and
until 10pm on Sundays, and they even
do vegetarian and vegan versions.

However, Jesse is most proud of
their soda bread, which he describes as
'remarkable'. Also spectacular is their
smoked salmon, bought from The Fish
Shop at Kensington Place and smoked
in-house at Parlour. The Fish Shop love

it so much that they ask Parlour to smoke
their salmon for them.

For Jesse, Parlour frees him from
the shackles of fine dining, allowing him
to create something he feels is more real
and inclusive. 'You can just come here
for a cup of coffee, or for a gastronomic
experience,' says Jesse.

Tables fill up with young families
and their newborns, or with laptops on
weekdays, and groups of friends looking
for a boozier brunch on the weekends.
Newspapers are available to browse, and
there's even a table dedicated to various
homemade breads for you to toast
yourself, along with jams and spreads
to go to town on. Sip on Parlour's own
lemon barley water, homemade iced tea
and Allpress coffee.

Parlour's Famous Soda Bread

From Parlour

MAKES AROUND THREE
SMALL LOAVES

190g plain flour
60g porridge oats
8g salt
8g bicarbonate
15g soft brown sugar
190g buttermilk
25g black treacle

This soda bread is not only quick and easy, but the homemade touch is sure to impress. It's delicious eaten alone, with various spreads, or as the perfect accompaniment to any breakfast dish – particularly with smoked salmon and scrambled eggs. Be careful not to over-work the dough.

Mix all the ingredients together thoroughly until you can roll it into a ball. Form the dough into round loaves and cut deep (around half-way into the dough) quarter sections – it should look like a cross. Spray with water, then dust heavily with flour. Bake at 220°C/gas 7 with a low fan (or better still, no fan) so the flour doesn't get blown off, for around 17–20 minutes.

You can make a bigger loaf or more loaves if you wish by multiplying the ingredients. Once the dough is made, it keeps very well for up to 5 days if you roll it into a ball and put it in the fridge well-covered in cling film. Take it out and bake when needed and you'll find it comes up fresh as a daisy.

BREAKFAST LONDON

La Crêperie de Hampstead

<u>77A Hampstead High St</u> <u>NW3 1RE</u>

One of London's best crêperies isn't somewhere you can make a reservation, sit down inside or hang around in. At the corner of Hampstead High Street and Perrin's Lane, La Crêperie de Hampstead is a little stall that has served sweet crêpes and savoury galettes since 1980.

On weekends, queues can extend down the street, but those standing eagerly in line know that it's worth waiting for. The stall has become an unofficial landmark of the area, and the cone wrappers holding the freshly made meal – featuring their iconic logo resembling a French street sign – are habitually photographed by customers and uploaded to social media.

The extensive menus offer a selection of combinations. Sweet crêpes offer a choice between milk, dark or white Belgian chocolate, with the option to mix them at extra cost. Popular choices include the garlic mushroom, cheese and ham galette and the hazelnut cream crunch crêpe.

La Crêperie de Hampstead is cash only, and is closed Mondays and Tuesdays.

Leyas

20 Camden High St
NW1 0JH

saintespresso.com

Right on Camden High Street, Leyas offers breakfast and artisan pastries alongside specialty coffee from a rotating variety of blends and roasteries.

The spot sees high amounts of take-aways daily, with customers stopping by for their caffeine and pastry fix. Others grab a table down in the basement seating area, playing a game of Scrabble from the café's board game selection, or setting up their laptop for a couple of hours of work.

Beside the steps leading up to the counter area (where you order from), the wall is painted with an eye-catching cartoon mural. The basement features monthly art exhibitions, and is furnished with wooden tables, chairs and Chesterfield sofas.

The menu considers all customers, offering vegetarian, vegan and gluten-free options. The eggs royale and avocado, chilli and lemon on toast are popular, as well as their toasted croissants. Be sure to take home their mousse-like brownie.

The Coffee Jar

83 Parkway
NW1 7PP

The Coffee Jar is a favourite amongst Camden locals, with many nearby residents habitually popping in to order their usual.

The first thing you'll notice about the white-fronted store is the abundant counter spread of pastries, cake and other treats, visible through the floor-to-ceiling windows. Next, it will be the use of reclaimed wood throughout the cosy café, as well as the exhibiting artwork hanging on the walls.

The morning menu is small, and the café is ideal for those after a caffeine kick and some baked goods, whether that's a stuffed ham, cheese and tomato croissant, a blueberry and ricotta muffin, or a slice of banana bread. Their humble avocado toast topped with sliced fresh tomatoes and basil pesto is also a popular order.

Monmouth is the café's house coffee of choice, with guest beans changing regularly to suit every palate.

BEST FOR...

Special occasions

The Delaunay, WC (p.17)
The Modern Pantry, EC (p.76)
Bourne & Hollingsworth Buildings,
    EC (p.83)
Duck & Waffle, EC (p.90)
Hawksmoor Guildhall, EC (p.96)
Aqua Shard, SE (p.142)
NAC, W (p.196)
NOPI, W (p.200)
The Wolseley, W (p.210)
Berners Tavern, W (p.219)

Vegans

The Haberdashery, N (p.44)
Friends of Ours, N (p.68)
Polo Bar, EC (p.80)
Cereal Killer Café, E (p.102)
I Will Kill Again, E (p.112)
MOTHER, E (p.120)
The Full Nelson, SE (p.138)
Where The Pancakes Are, SE (p.140)
Farm Girl, SW (p.183)
Golborne Deli & Bistro, W (p.212)
The Fields Beneath, NW (p.232)
LLS Café, NW (p.236)

Global palettes

Hungover indulgence

Insta-worthy breakfasts and brunches

Grab-and-go

Boozy brunches

Fink's Salt & Sweet, N (p.54)
100 Hoxton, N (p.62)
Friends of Ours, N (p.68)
Ozone Coffee, EC (p.82)
Bourne & Hollingsworth Buildings, EC (p.83)
Ask for Janice, EC (p.88)
Hawksmoor Guildhall, EC (p.96)
Flotsam & Jetsam, SW (p.176)
Mac & Wild, W (p.208)
Pachamama, W (p.214)

Weekday working

Store St Espresso, WC (p.14)
Timberyard, WC (p.24)
Look Mum No Hands!, EC (p.86)
Attendant, EC (p.89)
Good & Proper Tea, EC (p.97)
White Mulberries, E (p.115)
Wood Street Coffee, E (p.133)
Brick House, SE (p.154)
Local Hero, SW (p.169)
Leyas, NW (p.244)

All-day breakfast (or until the kitchen closes)

Brunswick East, N (p.46)
Polo Bar, EC (p.80)
Attendant, EC (p.89)
Good & Proper Tea, EC (p.97)
TRADE, E (p.129)
Where The Pancakes Are, SE (p.140)
Brother Marcus, SW (p.164)
Flotsam & Jetsam, SW (p.176)
Tried & True, SW (p.179)
Burnt Toast Café, SW (p.185)
Urban Pantry, W (p.220)
Café Loren, NW (p.229)
LLS Café, NW (p.236)

Families with young children

Banner's, N (p.45)
Toconoco, N (p.67)
Wood Street Coffee, E (p.133)
Where The Pancakes Are, SE (p.140)
Vanilla Black Coffee & Books, SE (p.148)
Flotsam & Jetsam, SW (p.176)
Tried & True, SW (p.179)
Angie's Little Food Shop, W (p.195)
Urban Pantry, W (p.220)
Ginger & White, NW (p.226)
Parlour, NW (p.238)

Index

Page references in *italics* indicate images.

Thank You

Thank you to the cafés, coffee shops, greasy spoons and restaurants – not just in this book, but all over London – that make this city's food scene worth writing about and celebrating every single day.

To my agent Claudia Young who shared my vision for the book, Elen Jones from Ebury Press who made it happen, and Laura Marchant who coordinated and guided me through each anxious and excited step of the way – all of whom I appreciate and thank immensely.

To Ben Gardiner and Lucy Sykes-Thompson for the book's beautiful design, and to Liz Marvin, our fantastic copy-editor.

To Mark McWilliams, whose stunning photography graces many pages, brilliantly editing all of the imagery to bring the book to life.

To my eternally, unconditionally supportive parents, Guy and Yee Chen, and my sister Ming, who inspire me to think big and are forever my biggest cheerleaders.

To Luke Grob, my support system, personal driver and late night toastie-maker, for endless encouragement when I most needed it.

And last but not least, to every follower and fan of Breakfast London, without whom this book would not exist.

Picture Credits

The following photos are © Mark McWilliams: p.18 (bottom picture), p.19, p.26, p.27, p.28/29, p.31, p.42, p.43, p.46, p.47, p.48/49, p.54/55, p.56, p.57, p.58, p.64, p.65, p.68, p.69, p.71, p.76, p.77, p.78/79, p.80/81, p.86, p.87, p.90 (top picture), p.91, p.92/93, p.94, p102/103, p.104, p.105, p.108, p.109, p.110/111, p.114, p.115, p.142, p.143, p.145, p.164, p.165, p.166/167, p.169, p.172, p.174, p.178, p.184, p.185, p.190, p.191, p.192/193, p.200, p.201, p.202/203, p.204, p.218/219, p.230, p.231, p.238, p.239, p.240, p.242, p.243.

All other photos © Bianca Bridges.

10 9 8 7 6 5 4 3 2 1

Ebury Press, an imprint of Ebury Publishing,
20 Vauxhall Bridge Road,
London
SW1V 2SA

Ebury Press is part of the Penguin Random House group of companies whose addresses
can be found at global.penguinrandomhouse.com

Penguin
Random House
UK

Copyright © Bianca Bridges 2019

Bianca Bridges has asserted her right to be identified as the author of this Work
in accordance with the Copyright, Designs and Patents Act 1988

Recipes reproduced with permission of respective restaurants.

Book Design: Ben Gardiner and Studio Polka
Photography: Mark McWilliams and Bianca Bridges
Project Editor: Laura Marchant
Copy-editor: Liz Marvin

First published in the United Kingdom by Ebury in 2019

A CIP catalogue record for this book is available from the British Library

ISBN 9781529102628

Colour origination by Rhapsody Media
Printed and bound in China by C&C Offest Printing Co., Ltd

Penguin Random House is committed to a sustainable future for our business, our readers
and our planet. This book is made from Forest Stewardship Council® certified paper.

We have taken all reasonable care to ensure that restaurant information is
accurate at the date of going to print. We apologise for any unintentional
omissions or errors, but in a fast-paced city like London, it's hard to keep
up. Please be sure to check opening hours and other information before you
visit your breakfast spot.